JAVASCRIPT
IN A NUTSHELL

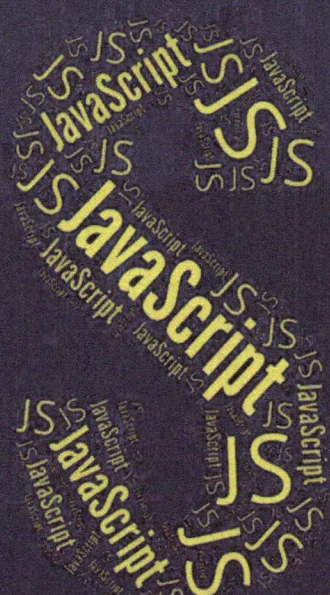

A Practical Guide
To Master JavaScript

David Mark

Copyright © 2024 David Mark All rights reserved

No part of this book may be reproduced, or stored in a retrieval system, or transmitted in any form or by any means, electronic, mechanical, photocopying, recording, or otherwise, without express written permission of the publisher.

ISBN: 979-8-3255-8058-1

Table of Contents

Introduction 1
   Key Features of JavaScript 1
   Applications of JavaScript 1
   Reasons to Learn JavaScript 2
   Development tools: 2
   Extensions for Visual Studio Code: 3
      Live Server: 3
      Code Formatting with Prettier 3
      Customizing Prettier Settings: 4
First Project 5
   Using Live Server 5
   Separating JavaScript from HTML 6
   The JavaScript Sandbox 7
   The JavaScript Console 7
      Logging Messages to the Console 7
      Debugging Your Code 8
      Logging Multiple Values 9
      Clearing the Console 9
      Logging Variables and Results 9
      Console Extensions 10
      Other Console Methods 10
      Styling Console Logs 10

- Commenting Code...11
- VScode Keyboard Shortcuts...11
  - Using Multiple Cursors..12
  - Searching for Files and Text......................................12
  - Toggling the Sidebar..13
- Variables and Variable Declarations......................................14
  - Variable Naming Conventions...14
  - Variable Formatting..15
  - Variable Reassignment...15
  - Arrays and Objects...15
  - Multiple Variable Declarations.......................................17
- Data Types in JavaScript...18
  - Primitive Data Types...18
  - Reference Types (Objects)..18
  - Dynamic Typing...19
    - Benefits of Dynamic Typing......................................19
    - Drawbacks of Dynamic Typing.................................19
  - Primitive Types..20
  - Reference Types..20
  - Null and Undefined...21
  - Type Checking..21
  - Memory Management...21
    - Stack...22
    - Heap..22
    - Primitive Types Reassignment................................22

- Reference Types and Reassignment..................23
- Type Conversion: Explicit and Implicit..................24
  - Explicit Type Conversion..................24
  - Implicit Type Conversion (Type Coercion)..................24
  - Temporary Object Wrappers..................25
  - Converting Strings to Decimals..................25
  - Converting Numbers to Booleans..................25
  - NaN (Not a Number)..................26
- Arithmetic Operators..................27
  - Concatenation Operator..................27
  - Exponent Operator..................27
  - Increment and Decrement Operators..................28
  - Assignment Operators..................28
  - Comparison Operators..................29
  - Triple Equals Operator (===)..................29
  - Not Equals Operator (!=)..................30
  - Not Equal Value or Not Equal Type Operator (!==)..................30
  - Greater Than (>) and Less Than (<) Operators..................30
  - Greater Than or Equal To (>=) and Less Than or Equal To (<=) Operators..................31
  - Type Coercion..................31
- String..................33
  - String Concatenation and Template Literals..................33
  - String Properties and Methods..................33
  - Accessing Individual Characters and Prototype..................34
  - String Properties and Methods..................35

- Substring and Slice 35
- Trim 36
- Replace 36
- Includes 36
- valueOf() 37
- Split 37
- Challenge: Capitalize 37
  - Solution 1: 38
  - Solution 2: 38
  - Solution 3: 38

Number 40

- Number Objects 40
- Converting Numbers to Strings 40
- Getting the Length of a Number 40
- Formatting Numbers with toFixed() 40
- toFixed() vs. toPrecision() 41
- toExponential() 41
- toLocaleString() 41
- Number Properties 41
  - Number.MAX_VALUE 41
  - Number.MIN_VALUE 42
  - Number.NaN 42
- Math Methods 42
  - Math.abs() 42
  - Math.round() 42

- Math.ceil()..42
- Math.floor()...42
- Math.pow()..43
- Math.min() and Math.max()................................43
- Math.random()..43
- Challenge: Random Number Operations..............43

Dates and Times..45
- Creating a Date Object..45
- Converting to a String...45
- Setting a Specific Date..45
- Setting a Specific Time..45
- Setting a Date and Time Using a String..............46
- Timestamps..46
  - Getting a Timestamp....................................46
  - Getting a Timestamp for a Specific Date.....46
  - Creating a Date Object from a Timestamp..47
  - Converting Timestamps to Seconds............47
- Getting Specific Date Parts.................................47
- Getting Specific Time Parts.................................47
- Creating Dates from Specific Parts.....................48
- Formatting Dates with Intl.DateTimeFormat.......48
- Shorter Syntax Using toLocaleString()................49

Arrays...50
- Creating Arrays..50
- Accessing Array Elements...................................50

- Manipulating Arrays...51
  - Accessing and Changing Elements..........................51
  - Adding Elements...51
  - Removing Elements..52
  - Getting the Length...52
- Array Methods...53
  - Mutating Methods..53
  - Non-Mutating Methods..53
- indexOf() and slice()..54
- splice()..55
- Nesting Arrays..56
- Concatenating Arrays...56
- Spread Operator...57
- Spread Operator vs. concat()..57
- Flattening Arrays...58
- Static Methods on the Array Object............................58
- Array Challenges..59
  - Challenge 1..59
  - Challenge 2..59

Object Literals...61
- Accessing and Modifying Object Properties..............61
- Object Keys with Multiple Words.................................63
- Spread Operator with Objects......................................63
- Object Constructor..64
- Custom Constructors..64

- Nesting Objects 65
- Object.assign() 65
- Arrays of Objects 65
  - Accessing Object Properties 66
  - Object.keys() 66
  - Object.values() 66
  - Object.entries() 66
  - Object.entries() and Object.hasOwnProperty() 66
- Shorthand Object Properties 67
- Destructuring 67
- Destructuring Nested Objects and Arrays 67
- Destructuring Arrays 68
- JSON (JavaScript Object Notation) 68
- Converting JavaScript Objects to JSON 69
- Using JSON with Local Storage 70
- JSON Arrays 70
- Accessing JSON Properties 71
- Object Challenge 71
  - Create an Array of Objects 71
  - Set the read Value to True for All Books 72
  - Destructure the Title from the First Book 73
  - Destructure the Title from the First Book 73
  - Convert the Library Object to a JSON String 73
- Functions and Scope 74
  - Creating Functions 74

Passing Data to Functions...75

Returning Values from Functions..75

Arguments and Parameters..75

    Default Parameters..76

    Rest Parameters..77

    Object Parameters..77

    Arrays as Parameters...78

    Rest Parameters and Arrays..78

Scope...79

    Global Scope...79

    Function Scope...80

    Local Scope...80

    Variable Shadowing...81

    VAR vs. LET and CONST..82

        VAR is Function Scoped..83

        Nested Functions and Nested Blocks..................................84

Function Expressions..86

Hoisting...86

    Function Declarations vs Function Expressions.......................87

Arrow Functions..87

    Implicit Return...88

    Lexical Scope..88

    Single Parameter...89

    Returning Objects..89

    Arrow Functions in Callbacks...89

- Advantages of Arrow Functions in Callbacks............89
- Immediately Invoked Function Expressions (IIFEs) 90
- Advantages of IIFEs...91
- Recursion..91
- Infinite Loops...92
- Execution Context..95
  - Global Execution Context..95
  - Function Execution Context..95
  - Memory Creation Phase..95
  - Execution Phase..96
  - Execution Context: Step-by-Step Walkthrough...........97
  - Execution Context: Call Stack......................................98
- Control Flow with If Statements.......................................101
  - Comparison Operators..101
  - Scope in If Statements..102
  - Shorthand If Statements...102
  - Else If Statements...102
  - Nested If Statements..103
  - Multiple Conditions in a Single If Statement...........104
- Switches..106
- Calculator Challenge..108
  - Solution using a switch statement:............................108
- Truthy and Falsy Values..110
  - Loose Equality (==) vs. Strict Equality (===)...............114
  - AND (&&)..114

- OR (||) 114
  - Conditional Rendering with AND (&&) 115
  - OR (||) and Nullish Coalescing Operator (??) 115
    - Logical Assignment Operators 116
  - OR Assignment (||=) 116
  - AND Assignment (&&=) 116
  - Nullish Coalescing Assignment (??=) 116
- Ternary Operator 118
  - Ternary Operator with Multiple Statements 119
  - Ternary Operator with Shorthand 119
- For Loop 121
  - Nested Loops 122
  - Break and Continue Statements 123
- While and Do-While Loops 125
  - Using While Loops with Arrays 125
  - Nested While Loops 126
  - When to Use Do-While Loops 126
- FizzBuzz Challenge 127
  - Solution (Using a For Loop): 127
  - Solution (Using a While Loop): 127
  - Solution (Using a For Loop): 128
  - Shorter Solution Using Modulus 15: 128
- For-Of Loop 130
  - Example (Iterating over an Array): 130
  - Example (Iterating over an Array of Objects): 130

- Example (Iterating over a String): 131
- High-Order Array Methods 132
  - forEach() 132
    - forEach() with Additional Parameters 133
    - Named Callback Functions 134
    - forEach() with Objects 134
  - filter() 135
    - filter() with Complex Objects 136
  - map() with Complex Objects 137
    - map() with Arrays of Objects 140
    - Chaining map() Methods 141
  - Chaining Different Methods 142
  - Reduce Method 143
    - Setting the Initial Value 144
    - For Loop Equivalent 145
    - Reduce Method vs. For Loop 145
- Challenge 147
  - Create an Array of Young People 147
  - Add All Positive Numbers 148
  - Capitalize First Letter of Words 149
- Introduction to the Document Object Model (DOM) 151
  - What is the DOM? 151
  - Importance of Understanding the DOM 151
  - What We Will Learn in This Section 151
  - The DOM Tree Structure 151

Accessing the DOM......152
Properties and Methods of the Document Object......153
    Accessing the Body and Its Contents......153
    Modifying the Body......153
    Accessing Links......154
    Writing to the Document......154
Selecting Elements by ID......155
Selecting Elements by Query Selector......156
Accessing Element Attributes......158
Accessing Element Classes......160
Accessing HTML Collections......161
Getting and Setting Attributes......162
Manipulating Element Content and Styles......163
Query Selector......165
Query Selector All......166
    Node Lists vs HTML Collections......168
    Converting HTML Collections to Arrays......169
Traversing the DOM: Parent, Child, and Sibling Relationships   170
    Modifying Elements and Traversing the DOM......171
    Traversing the DOM: Sibling Elements......172
    Traversing the DOM: Other Node Types......173
    Traversing the DOM: Child Nodes......174
    Comments as Nodes......174
    Accessing Node Properties......175
    Accessing Parent Nodes......176

- Accessing Siblings...177
- Creating Elements..177
- Adding Content to Elements...178
  - Creating a Function to Add List Items....................................179
- Creating Reusable Functions for Elements...................................181
- Inserting Elements into the DOM..184
  - Insert Adjacent Element..184
  - Insert Adjacent Text...184
  - insertBefore() Method...185
  - Comparison of insertAdjacent and insertBefore.....................186
- Replacing Elements in the DOM..188
  - Replacing a Specific Item..190
  - Replacing an Element with a New Element............................191
- Removing Elements...193
  - Removing a Specific Item from a List.....................................194

Manipulating CSS Classes and Styles...196
- Manipulating CSS Classes with classList....................................197
- Styling Elements with style Property..198
- Looping Through Elements and Styling.......................................199

Event Listeners..200
- Recommended Method: addEventListener()...............................200
- Multiple Event Listeners..201
- Multiple Event Listeners with Different Actions.........................201
- Synchronous vs. Asynchronous Execution...................................202
- Named Callback Functions..202

- Removing Event Listeners 202
- Triggering Events Programmatically 202
- Clearing Items from a List 203
- Other Mouse Events 203
  - Double Click 204
  - Context Menu 204
  - Mouse Over and Mouse Out 204
  - Mouse Move 205
  - Right Click 205
  - Mouse Down and Mouse Up 205
  - Mouse Wheel 205
  - Mouse Over and Mouse Out 206
  - Drag Start 206
  - Drag and Drag End 206
- Event Object 206
  - Target vs. Current Target 207
  - Other Event Object Properties 208
  - Mouse Coordinates 208
  - Preventing Default Behavior 208
  - Dynamic Event Values 209
- Keyboard Events 210
  - Key Properties 210
  - Modifier Keys 211
  - Using Modifier Keys with Key Codes 212
  - Building a Key Code Info Application 212

- Dynamically Creating Display Elements........................214
- Handling the Space Key......................................215
- Creating Display Elements Dynamically Using an Object Map 215
- Creating Display Elements Dynamically Using Text Nodes 216
- Handling Input Events..217
- Retrieving Input Values Using Event Listeners.......217
- Updating the Display Dynamically......................218
- Retrieving Values from Select Lists and Checkboxes 218
- Focus and Blur Events...219
- Styling Input Elements with Focus and Blur..............219
- Preventing Form Submission..................................220
- Form Validation and Data Retrieval......................220
- Event Bubbling..222
- Event Delegation...224
- Window Events...226

Introduction

JavaScript is a high-level, interpreted programming language that plays a crucial role in web development. It complements HTML, which structures web page content, and CSS, which styles that content. JavaScript brings life to the user interface of websites and web applications, making them dynamic and interactive.

Key Features of JavaScript

- **Interpreted:** JavaScript code is executed line by line, making it a scripting language.
- **Dynamic:** JavaScript allows for dynamic changes to the Document Object Model (DOM), the tree-like structure of elements on a web page.
- **Event Handling:** JavaScript enables developers to respond to user actions, such as mouse clicks, keyboard events, and form submissions.
- **Asynchronous Requests:** JavaScript can make HTTP requests to interact with back-end servers, allowing for data exchange and dynamic updates.

Applications of JavaScript

JavaScript is widely used for:

- Manipulating the DOM to change content, styles, and structure.
- Handling user events to create interactive interfaces.
- Making asynchronous requests to fetch or submit data from servers.
- Building complex web applications with features like modals, dropdowns, and collapsible content.

Beyond the basics, JavaScript offers a wide range of advanced capabilities:

- **Animations and Effects:** JavaScript enables the creation of dynamic animations and effects using CSS transitions, request animation frame, and libraries like animate.css and gsap.
- **Data Manipulation:** JavaScript provides data structures like arrays, allowing for sorting, filtering, and aggregation of data using powerful array methods like `map`, `filter`, and `reduce`.
- **Data Storage:** JavaScript can store data on the client-side using local storage, session storage, and cookies.
- **Single Page Applications (SPAs):** JavaScript enables the creation of SPAs that load a single HTML page and dynamically update content without reloading the entire page, providing a seamless user experience.
- **Server-Side Development:** With the Node.js runtime, JavaScript can be used on the server-side to interact with databases, create APIs, and handle file system operations.

Reasons to Learn JavaScript

- **Popularity:** JavaScript is one of the most widely used programming languages, offering ample job opportunities and collaboration possibilities.
- **Versatility:** JavaScript can be used for both front-end and back-end development, making it a full-stack language.
- **Ease of Learning:** Compared to low-level compiled languages, JavaScript is relatively easy to learn, making it accessible to a wide range of developers.
- **Large Community:** JavaScript has a vast and active community, providing abundant resources, support, and tools for learning and development.

Development tools:

- **Text Editor:** Visual Studio Code is a popular and user-friendly text editor with excellent extensions for web development.
- **Version Control:** Git is a version control system that allows you to track changes to your code and collaborate with others.

- **Node.js:** Node.js is a JavaScript runtime that enables you to run JavaScript on your machine or server.
- **npm:** npm is the Node.js package manager, which provides access to a vast repository of open-source JavaScript packages.

Extensions for Visual Studio Code:

- **Live Server:** This extension provides a mini development server that automatically reloads your browser when you make changes to your code.
- **Prettier:** This extension formats your code automatically, keeping it clean and consistent.

Live Server:

1. Open Visual Studio Code.
2. Click on the Extensions icon in the left sidebar.
3. Search for "Live Server".
4. Click on the "Install" button.

Once installed, you can use Live Server by opening a folder containing your JavaScript files and clicking on the "Go Live" button in the status bar. This will start a local server and automatically reload your browser when you make changes to your code.

Code Formatting with Prettier

Prettier is a code formatter that automatically formats your JavaScript code according to a set of rules. This helps to keep your code clean, consistent, and easy to read.

To format your code with Prettier, you can use the following steps:

1. Install the Prettier extension in Visual Studio Code.
2. Open your JavaScript file in Visual Studio Code.
3. Go to the **Settings** menu (Ctrl + , on Windows/Linux, Cmd + , on macOS).
4. Search for "Prettier".

5. Enable the **Format on Save** option.

Customizing Prettier Settings:

You can customize Prettier's settings to match your preferences. For example, you can choose to use single or double quotes, and you can set the tab width.

To customize Prettier's settings:

1. Go to the **Settings** menu (Ctrl + , on Windows/Linux, Cmd + , on macOS).
2. Search for "Prettier".
3. Adjust the settings as desired.

To set Prettier to use single quotes and a tab width of 2:

1. Go to the **Settings** menu (Ctrl + , on Windows/Linux, Cmd + , on macOS).
2. Search for "Prettier".
3. Check the **Single Quote** checkbox.
4. Set the **Tab Width** to 2.

Note: You can also format your code manually by pressing `Ctrl + Shift + P` (Windows/Linux) or `Cmd + Shift + P` (macOS) and selecting **Format Document**.

First Project

To create an HTML file and run JavaScript in it, you can follow these steps:

1. Create a new file in your text editor and save it with a `.html` extension.
2. Add the following code to the file:

```html
<!DOCTYPE html>
<html>
<head>
  <title>My Website</title>
</head>
<body>
  <h1>Hello World</h1>

  <script>
    alert("Hello");
  </script>
</body>
</html>
```

3. Open the HTML file in a web browser.
4. You should see an alert box with the message "Hello".

Using Live Server

Live Server is a tool that automatically reloads your web page when you make changes to your code. This can be helpful for development, as you don't have to manually reload the page every time you make a change.

To use Live Server, you can follow these steps:

1. Install the Live Server extension in Visual Studio Code.
2. Open your HTML file in Visual Studio Code.

3. Click the **Go Live** button in the bottom right corner of the window.
4. Your web page will open in a new tab in your browser.
5. Any changes you make to your code will be automatically reloaded in the browser.

If you change the message in the `alert()` function to "Hello World", Live Server will automatically reload the page and display the new message in the alert box.

Separating JavaScript from HTML

It is considered bad practice to write JavaScript directly in your HTML file. Instead, it is better to create a separate JavaScript file and link it to your HTML file. This makes your code more organized and easier to maintain.

To create a separate JavaScript file, you can follow these steps:

1. Create a new file in your text editor and save it with a `.js` extension.
2. Write your JavaScript code in the file.
3. Link the JavaScript file to your HTML file using the `<script>` tag.

For example, you could create a file called `script.js` with the following code:

```
alert("Hello from the JS file");
```

Then, you could link the `script.js` file to your HTML file using the following code:

```
<script src="script.js"></script>
```

Note: The `src` attribute of the `<script>` tag specifies the path to the JavaScript file.

If you save the `script.js` file in the same folder as your HTML file, and you add the `<script>` tag to your HTML file, you should see an alert box with the message "Hello from the JS file" when you open the HTML file in a web browser.

The JavaScript Sandbox

The JavaScript sandbox is a tool that allows you to experiment with JavaScript code without having to create a full web page. This can be helpful for learning JavaScript, as you can quickly test out different code snippets without having to worry about the rest of the page.

To use the JavaScript sandbox, you can follow these steps:

1. Open the JavaScript sandbox in your web browser.
2. Write your JavaScript code in the editor.
3. Click the **Run** button to execute your code.

Note: The JavaScript sandbox is a great way to learn JavaScript, but it is important to remember that it is not a substitute for a full development environment. When you are developing real-world applications, you will need to use a text editor and a web server to create and run your code.

The JavaScript Console

The JavaScript console is a tool that allows you to interact with your JavaScript code and debug your web pages. It is available in all major web browsers, and can be accessed by pressing `Ctrl+Shift+J` (Windows) or `Cmd+Option+J` (Mac).

The console can be used to:

- Log messages to the console.
- Display warnings and errors.
- Evaluate JavaScript expressions.
- Debug your code.

Logging Messages to the Console

To log a message to the console, you can use the `console.log()` function. For example, the following code will log the message "Hello, world!" to the console:

```
console.log("Hello, world!");
```

The console will also display warnings and errors that occur in your JavaScript code. For example, if you try to access a property of an undefined variable, you will see a warning in the console.

You can also use the console to evaluate JavaScript expressions. For example, the following code will evaluate the expression 1 + 1 and log the result to the console:

```
console.log(1 + 1); // 2
```

Debugging Your Code

The console can be a valuable tool for debugging your JavaScript code. You can use the console to:

- Set breakpoints to stop the execution of your code at specific points.
- Step through your code line by line.
- Inspect the values of variables.

In the following example, we will use the console to debug a JavaScript function that is not working as expected:

```
function addNumbers(a, b) {
   return a + b;
}

console.log(addNumbers(1, 2)); // 3
console.log(addNumbers(3, 4)); // 7
console.log(addNumbers("1", "2")); // "12"
```

In this example, the `addNumbers()` function is not working as expected because it is concatenating the two input strings instead of adding them. We can use the console to debug this issue by setting a breakpoint at the line where the function is called. This will allow us to inspect the values of the input variables and the return value of the function.

Once we have identified the issue, we can fix the function by using the `parseInt()` function to convert the input strings to numbers before adding them.

```
function addNumbers(a, b) {
   return parseInt(a) + parseInt(b);
}

console.log(addNumbers(1, 2)); // 3
console.log(addNumbers(3, 4)); // 7
console.log(addNumbers("1", "2")); // 3
```

Logging Multiple Values

We can log multiple values to the console at the same time by passing them as arguments to the `console.log()` function. For example, the following code will log the number 100, the string "Hello, world!", and the Boolean value `true` to the console:

```
console.log(100, "Hello, world!", true);
```

The output in the console will look like this:

```
100 Hello, world! true
```

Clearing the Console

We can clear the console using the `clear()` function. For example, the following code will clear the console:

```
console.clear();
```

Logging Variables and Results

We will often log variables or the results of functions to the console. It is less common to log strings directly, unless we are displaying a message like "It worked!" after running a function.

To log a variable, we can simply use the `console.log()` function and pass the variable as an argument. For example, the following code will log the value of the variable x to the console:

```
let x = 100;
console.log(x);
```

Console Extensions

There are several extensions available for the JavaScript console that can make it easier to use. One popular extension is the "ES6 Code Snippets" extension, which provides snippets for common tasks like logging, debugging, and creating objects.

To use the "ES6 Code Snippets" extension, simply install it from the Chrome Web Store. Once installed, you can access the snippets by typing the shortcut key (usually `Ctrl + Space`) in the console.

Other Console Methods

In addition to `console.log()`, there are several other methods available on the `console` object. These methods include:

- `console.error()`: Logs a message to the console with a red background and border.
- `console.warn()`: Logs a message to the console with a yellow background.
- `console.table()`: Logs an object as a table.
- `console.group()`: Starts a group of messages.
- `console.groupEnd()`: Ends a group of messages.

Styling Console Logs

We can add CSS styles to our console logs using the `console.log()` method. To do this, we create a variable with the desired styles and then pass the variable as the second argument to `console.log()`.

For example, the following code will log the string "Hello, world!" to the console with a green text color and a white background:

```javascript
const styles = {
  color: 'green',
  backgroundColor: 'white',
  padding: '10px'
};

console.log('%cHello, world!', styles);
```

Commenting Code

Comments are used to document code and explain things in a more human-readable way. They are especially important when working on a project with a team of developers. Comments can also be used to disable code or to create a to-do list for yourself or other developers.

To create a single-line comment in JavaScript, simply add two forward slashes (//) to the beginning of the line. For example:

```javascript
// This is a single-line comment.
```

To create a multi-line comment, use the following syntax:

```javascript
/*
This is a multi-line comment.
*/
```

VScode Keyboard Shortcuts

There are several keyboard shortcuts that can be used to navigate and edit code in JavaScript. Some of the most useful shortcuts include:

- **Command/Control + /:** Toggle a single-line comment.
- **Command/Control + Shift + /:** Toggle a multi-line comment.
- **Command/Control + Right Arrow:** Move the cursor to the end of the line.
- **Command/Control + Left Arrow:** Move the cursor to the beginning of the line.
- **Command/Control + Up Arrow:** Move the cursor to the previous line.
- **Command/Control + Down Arrow:** Move the cursor to the next line.
- **Shift + Up Arrow/Down Arrow:** Highlight multiple lines of code.
- **Shift + Right Arrow/Left Arrow:** Highlight multiple characters on the same line.
- **Option/Alt + Right Arrow/Left Arrow:** Move the cursor to the beginning or end of the current word.
- **Shift + Option/Alt + Right Arrow/Left Arrow:** Highlight multiple words.
- **Command/Control + Shift + O:** Open a file.
- **Command/Control + Option/Alt + F:** Find all occurrences of a string in the current file.
- **Command/Control + Shift + F:** Find all occurrences of a string in all files in the project.
- **Command/Control + Option/Alt + Up Arrow/Down Arrow:** Move the cursor to the previous or next occurrence of the current word.
- **Command/Control + Option/Alt + Click:** Place the cursor at the beginning or end of the current word.
- **Command/Control + Shift + L:** Select all occurrences of the current word.

Using Multiple Cursors

VS Code allows you to use multiple cursors to edit multiple lines of code at the same time. To place multiple cursors, hold down the **Option/Alt** key on Windows or **Command** key on Mac and click on the desired locations. You can then type to edit all of the selected lines simultaneously.

Searching for Files and Text

You can use the **Command/Control + Shift + O** shortcut to open a file.

To search for a string in the current file, use the **Command/Control + Option/Alt + F** shortcut.

To search for a string in all files in the project, use the **Command/Control + Shift + F** shortcut.

Toggling the Sidebar

To toggle the sidebar in VS Code, press the **Command/Control + Option/Alt + B** shortcut.

Variables and Variable Declarations

Variables are containers for pieces of data in JavaScript. To declare a variable, you can use one of three keywords: `var`, `let`, or `const`.

- **var:** The original variable declaration keyword. It is still supported but is not recommended for new code.
- **let:** Introduced in ES6, `let` is used to declare variables that are block-scoped. This means that they are only accessible within the block in which they are declared.
- **const:** Also introduced in ES6, `const` is used to declare constants. Constants are values that cannot be reassigned.

Variable Naming Conventions

When naming variables, there are a few conventions that you should follow:

- Variable names can only contain letters, numbers, underscores, and dollar signs.
- Variable names must start with a letter or an underscore.
- Variable names should be descriptive and easy to understand.
- It is common to use camelCase or snake_case for variable names.

Example
```javascript
// Declare a variable using `let`
let firstName = "John";

// Declare a variable using `const`
const age = 30;

// Log the values of the variables
console.log(firstName); // Output: John
console.log(age); // Output: 30
```

Note: It is important to initialize variables before using them. If you try to use a variable that has not been initialized, you will get an error.

Variable Formatting

There are several ways to format variable names in JavaScript:

- **Camel case:** The first word is lowercase, and subsequent words are capitalized. For example: `firstName`, `lastName`.
- **Snake case:** Words are separated by underscores. For example: `first_name`, `last_name`.
- **Pascal case:** The first letter of each word is capitalized. For example: `FirstName`, `LastName`.

Variable Reassignment

- **`let` variables:** Can be reassigned to new values.
- **`const` variables:** Cannot be reassigned.

Example

```
// Reassign a `let` variable
let age = 30;
age = 31;
console.log(age); // Output: 31

// Attempt to reassign a `const` variable
const x = 100;
x = 200; // Error: Assignment to constant variable
```

Note: You can declare a `let` variable without initializing it, but you cannot declare a `const` variable without initializing it.

Arrays and Objects

Arrays and objects are not primitive values. This means that when you assign an array or object to a variable, you are not actually assigning the array or object itself to the variable. Instead, you are assigning a reference to the array or object.

This means that you can reassign the variable to a new array or object, but you cannot directly modify the array or object that the variable is referencing.

For example:

```
// Create an array
const arr = [1, 2, 3];

// Reassign the variable to a new array
arr = [4, 5, 6];

// Attempt to modify the original array
arr[0] = 7; // Error: Cannot assign to read-only property
```

In this example, the `arr` variable is reassigned to a new array. However, the original array is not modified.

While `const` variables cannot be directly reassigned, you can still modify arrays and objects that are referenced by `const` variables.

To modify an array referenced by a `const` variable, you can use array methods such as `push()`, `pop()`, and `splice()`.

Example:

```
// Create an array and assign it to a `const` variable
const arr = [1, 2, 3];

// Modify the array using the `push()` method
arr.push(4);

// Log the modified array
console.log(arr); // Output: [1, 2, 3, 4]
```

To modify an object referenced by a `const` variable, you can use dot notation or bracket notation to access and modify its properties.

Example:

```javascript
// Create an object and assign it to a `const` variable
const person = { name: "Brad" };

// Modify the object using dot notation
person.name = "John";

// Log the modified object
console.log(person); // Output: { name: "John" }
```

Multiple Variable Declarations

You can declare multiple variables of the same type (either `let` or `const`) in a single statement, separated by commas.

Example:

```javascript
// Declare multiple `let` variables
let a, b, c;

// Declare multiple `const` variables
const d = 10, e = 20, f = 30;
```

Note: It is generally considered good practice to declare one variable per statement for clarity and readability.

Data Types in JavaScript

JavaScript has two main types of data types: primitive data types and reference types (objects).

Primitive Data Types

Primitive data types are immutable values that are stored directly in the variable. They include:

- **String:** A sequence of characters enclosed in quotes (single, double, or backticks).
- **Number:** An integer or floating-point number.
- **Boolean:** A logical value that can be either `true` or `false`.
- **Null:** Represents the intentional absence of a value.
- **Undefined:** Represents a variable that has not been defined or assigned.
- **Symbol:** A unique and immutable value that is used as an identifier.
- **BigInt:** A large integer that cannot be represented by the regular number type.

Example:

```javascript
// Primitive data types
const name = "Brad"; // String
const age = 30; // Number
const isMarried = true; // Boolean
const job = null; // Null
let salary; // Undefined
```

Reference Types (Objects)

Reference types are non-primitive values that are stored in memory and accessed by reference. They include:

- **Object:** A collection of key-value pairs.
- **Array:** An ordered collection of values.
- **Function:** A block of code that can be executed.

Example:

```javascript
// Reference types
const person = { name: "Brad", age: 30 }; // Object
const numbers = [1, 2, 3]; // Array
const greet = function() { console.log("Hello!"); }; // Function
```

Dynamic Typing

JavaScript is a dynamically typed language, meaning that the type of a variable is not explicitly defined. Instead, the type is determined by the value assigned to the variable. This is in contrast to statically typed languages, such as C++ or Java, where the type of a variable must be explicitly declared.

Example:

```javascript
let x = "Hello"; // x is a string
x = 10; // x is now a number
```

Benefits of Dynamic Typing

- **Simplicity:** Dynamic typing makes code easier to write and read, as you don't have to explicitly define the types of variables.
- **Flexibility:** Dynamic typing allows you to change the type of a variable at runtime, which can be useful in certain situations.

Drawbacks of Dynamic Typing

- **Errors:** Dynamic typing can lead to errors if you are not careful, as the type of a variable may not be what you expect.
- **Performance:** Static typing can improve performance in some cases, as the compiler can optimize code based on the known types of variables.

Tips and Tricks

- Use `const` for variables that you don't intend to reassign.
- Use keyboard shortcuts to speed up your workflow, such as `Shift + D` to select the next instance of a word.
- Use the `typeof` operator to check the type of a variable, especially when debugging.

Primitive Types

Primitive types are immutable values that are stored directly in the variable. They include:

- **Number:** Represents numeric values.
- **String:** Represents sequences of characters.
- **Boolean:** Represents true or false values.
- **Null:** Represents an intentional empty value.
- **Undefined:** Represents a variable that has not been assigned a value.
- **Symbol:** Represents unique identifiers.
- **BigInt:** Represents very large numbers.

Example:

```javascript
const name = "Brad"; // String
const age = 30; // Number
const hasKids = true; // Boolean
const apartmentNumber = null; // Null
let score; // Undefined
const id = Symbol("unique-id"); // Symbol
const bigNumber = 9007199254740991n; // BigInt
```

Reference Types

Reference types are mutable values that are stored in memory and accessed through a reference. They include:

- **Array:** Represents a collection of values.

- **Object:** Represents a collection of key-value pairs.
- **Function:** Represents a block of code that can be executed.

Example:

```javascript
const numbers = [1, 2, 3]; // Array
const person = { name: "Brad", age: 30 }; // Object
const sayHello = function() { console.log("Hello"); }; // Function
```

Null and Undefined

Null and undefined are both primitive types, but they have different meanings:

- **Null:** Represents an intentional empty value.
- **Undefined:** Represents a variable that has not been assigned a value.

Historically, null was incorrectly classified as an object type due to the way JavaScript values were represented in early implementations. However, null is not an object, and it is now considered a primitive type.

Type Checking

You can use the `typeof` operator to check the type of a variable.

Example:

```javascript
console.log(typeof name); // Logs "string"
console.log(typeof numbers); // Logs "object"
console.log(typeof sayHello); // Logs "function"
```

Memory Management

In JavaScript, data is stored in two areas of memory: the stack and the heap.

Stack

The stack is a memory area where primitive types are stored. Primitive types are immutable values that are stored directly in the variable.

Example:

```javascript
// Primitive types are stored on the stack
const name = "John";
const age = 30;
```

Heap

The heap is a memory area where reference types are stored. Reference types are mutable values that are stored in memory and accessed through a reference.

Example:

```javascript
// Reference types are stored on the heap
const person = { name: "Brad", age: 40 };
```

Primitive Types Reassignment

When you assign a primitive type to a variable, the value is copied into the variable.

Example:

```javascript
const newName = name; // newName is assigned a copy of the value of name
```

When you reassign a primitive type, the value of the variable is changed.

Example:

```javascript
newName = "Jonathan"; // newName is reassigned to a new value
```

Reference Types and Reassignment

Reference types are stored in the heap and accessed through a reference. When you assign a reference type to a variable, the variable stores a reference to the object in the heap.

Example:

```javascript
const person = { name: "Brad", age: 40 };
const newPerson = person; // newPerson is assigned a reference to the object stored in person
```

When you reassign a reference type, the variable still points to the same object in the heap.

Example:

```javascript
newPerson.name = "Bradley"; // The name property of the object pointed to by newPerson is changed
```

This means that changes made to the object through one variable will also be reflected in the other variable.

Example :

```javascript
// Reference types are stored on the heap
const person = { name: "Brad", age: 40 };
const new_person = person; // new_person is assigned a reference to the object stored in person

// Reassigning a reference type changes the object pointed to by the variable
new_person.name = "Bradley"; // The name property of the object pointed to by new_person is changed

// Changes made through one variable are reflected in the other variable
console.log(person.name); // Output: Bradley
console.log(new_person.name); // Output: Bradley
```

This behavior is different from primitive types, where the value is stored directly in the variable. When you reassign a primitive type, the value of the variable is changed, but the original value remains unchanged.

Type Conversion: Explicit and Implicit

Explicit Type Conversion

Explicit type conversion is the process of manually converting a value from one type to another.

Example:

```javascript
// Convert a string to a number using parseInt()
let amount = parseInt("100"); // amount is now a number

// Convert a number to a string using toString()
amount = amount.toString(); // amount is now a string
```

Implicit Type Conversion (Type Coercion)

Implicit type conversion, also known as type coercion, occurs when JavaScript automatically converts a value from one type to another. This can happen in certain operations, such as:

- **Arithmetic operations:** When an arithmetic operation is performed on values of different types, JavaScript will convert the values to a common type. For example, if you add a string and a number, JavaScript will convert the string to a number.
- **Assignment:** When a value is assigned to a variable of a different type, JavaScript will convert the value to the type of the variable.

Example:

```javascript
// Implicitly convert a string to a number in an arithmetic operation
const result = "100" + 10; // result is now a string ("10010")
```

```javascript
// Implicitly convert a number to a string in an assignment
const message = 100 + ""; // message is now a string ("100")
```

Implicit type conversion can sometimes lead to unexpected results, so it's important to be aware of how it works.

Temporary Object Wrappers

When you use a method on a primitive value, JavaScript creates a temporary object wrapper of the appropriate type. This allows you to access methods that are not normally available on primitive values.

Example:

```javascript
// Primitive value (number)
const num = 100;

// Use a method on the primitive value
const numString = num.toString(); // numString is now a string ("100")
```

This behavior can be confusing, but it's important to understand that the primitive value itself is not changed. The temporary object wrapper is created only for the duration of the operation.

Converting Strings to Decimals

To convert a string representing a decimal number to a decimal number, use the `parseFloat()` method.

Example:

```javascript
// Convert a string to a decimal using parseFloat()
const amount = parseFloat("99.5"); // amount is now a decimal number (99.5)
```

Converting Numbers to Booleans

The `Boolean()` constructor can be used to convert a number to a Boolean value. In JavaScript, truthy values (such as 1) are converted to `true`, while falsy values (such as 0) are converted to `false`.

Example:

```javascript
// Convert a number to a Boolean using the Boolean()
constructor
const isTrue = Boolean(1); // isTrue is now true
const isFalse = Boolean(0); // isFalse is now false
```

NaN (Not a Number)

NaN is a special value in JavaScript that represents "Not a Number". It is returned when a numeric operation cannot be performed, such as trying to convert a non-numeric string to a number.

Example:

```javascript
// Convert a non-numeric string to a number
const result = parseInt("hello"); // result is NaN
```

It's important to be aware of NaN and handle it appropriately in your code, as it can lead to unexpected results.

There are five ways to obtain NaN in JavaScript:

1. **Parsing a non-numeric string:**

   ```javascript
   const result = parseInt("hello"); // result is NaN
   ```

2. **Math operations with non-real results:**

   ```javascript
   const result = Math.sqrt(-1); // result is NaN
   ```

3. **Operand of an argument is NaN:**

   ```javascript
   const result = 1 + NaN; // result is NaN
   ```

4. **Undefined operands:**

   ```javascript
   const result = undefined + undefined; // result is NaN
   ```

5. **String operations (except addition):**

```js
const result = "foo" / 3; // result is NaN
```

Arithmetic Operators

Arithmetic operators perform mathematical operations on numbers. The most common arithmetic operators are:

- Addition (+)
- Subtraction (-)
- Multiplication (*)
- Division (/)
- Modulus (%) (returns the remainder of a division operation)

Example:

```
const x = 5;
console.log(x + 5); // 10
console.log(x - 5); // 0
console.log(x * 5); // 25
console.log(x / 5); // 1
console.log(x % 5); // 0
```

Concatenation Operator

The concatenation operator (+) can be used to combine strings together.

Example:

```
const hello = "Hello";
const world = "World";
console.log(hello + " " + world); // "Hello World"
```

Exponent Operator

The exponent operator (**) raises the first operand to the power of the second operand.

Example:

```
const x = 2;
console.log(x ** 3); // 8
```

Increment and Decrement Operators

- **Increment (++)**: Increments a number by 1.
- **Decrement (--)**: Decrements a number by 1.

Example:

```
let x = 1;
console.log(++x); // 2
console.log(--x); // 1
```

Assignment Operators

Assignment operators assign values to variables. They can be used with arithmetic operators to perform operations and assign the result to a variable.

- **Value assignment (=)**: Assigns a value to a variable.
- **Addition assignment (+=)**: Adds a value to a variable.
- **Subtraction assignment (-=)**: Subtracts a value from a variable.
- **Multiplication assignment (*=)**: Multiplies a variable by a value.
- **Division assignment (/=)**: Divides a variable by a value.
- **Modulus assignment (%=)**: Computes the remainder of dividing a variable by a value.
- **Exponent assignment (**=)**: Raises a variable to the power of a value.

Example:

```
let x = 10;
x += 5; // x is now 15
x -= 5; // x is now 10
```

Comparison Operators

Comparison operators compare two values and return a boolean result (true or false).

- **Equal to (==)**: Checks if two values are equal.
- **Equal value and equal type (===)**: Checks if two values are equal and of the same type.
- **Not equal to (!=)**: Checks if two values are not equal.
- **Not equal value or not equal type (!==)**: Checks if two values are not equal or not of the same type.
- **Greater than (>)**: Checks if the first value is greater than the second value.
- **Greater than or equal to (>=)**: Checks if the first value is greater than or equal to the second value.
- **Less than (<)**: Checks if the first value is less than the second value.
- **Less than or equal to (<=)**: Checks if the first value is less than or equal to the second value.

Example:

```
const x = 2;
console.log(x == 2); // true
console.log(x === 2); // true
console.log(x != 2); // false
console.log(x !== 2); // false
```

Triple Equals Operator (===)

The triple equals operator (===) checks if two values are equal and of the same type. It is recommended to use this operator over the double equals operator (==) to avoid potential type coercion issues.

Example:

```
const x = 2;
console.log(x === 2); // true
console.log(x === '2'); // false
```

Not Equals Operator (!=)

The not equals operator (!=) checks if two values are not equal. It is the opposite of the equals operator (==).

Example:

```
const x = 2;
console.log(x != 2); // false
console.log(x != '2'); // true
```

Not Equal Value or Not Equal Type Operator (!==)

The not equal value or not equal type operator (!==) checks if two values are not equal or not of the same type. It is the opposite of the triple equals operator (===).

Example:

```
const x = 2;
console.log(x !== 2); // false
console.log(x !== '2'); // true
```

Greater Than (>) and Less Than (<) Operators

The greater than (>) and less than (<) operators compare two values and return a boolean result (true or false).

Example:

```
const x = 10;
console.log(x > 5); // true
console.log(x < 5); // false
```

Greater Than or Equal To (>=) and Less Than or Equal To (<=) Operators

The greater than or equal to (>=) and less than or equal to (<=) operators compare two values and return a boolean result (true or false).

Example:

```
const x = 10;
console.log(x >= 5); // true
console.log(x <= 5); // false
```

Type Coercion

Type coercion is the implicit conversion of a value from one type to another. It can occur when operators are applied to values of different types.

Example:

```
const x = 5 + '5'; // x is now '55'
```

In this example, the plus operator coerces the number 5 to a string, resulting in the concatenation of the two strings.

Type coercion can occur in various scenarios:

- **Number and String Concatenation:** When a number is concatenated with a string, the number is coerced to a string.

Example:

```
const x = 5 + '5'; // x is now '55'
```

- **Multiplication of Number and String:** When a number is multiplied by a string, the string is coerced to a number.

Example:

```
const x = 5 * '5'; // x is now 25
```

- **Addition of Number and Null:** When a number is added to null, null is coerced to 0.

Example:

```
const x = 5 + null; // x is now 5
```

- **Number Conversion of Boolean Values:** True and false are coerced to 1 and 0, respectively, when used as numbers.

Example:

```
const x = 5 + true;  // x is now 6
const y = 5 + false; // y is now 5
```

- **Addition of Number and Undefined:** When a number is added to undefined, undefined is coerced to NaN.

Example:

```
const x = 5 + undefined; // x is now NaN
```

String

String Concatenation and Template Literals

String concatenation involves joining multiple strings together. In JavaScript, we can concatenate strings using the + operator.

Example:

```
const name = 'John';
const age = 30;
const greeting = 'Hello, my name is ' + name + ' and I am ' + age + ' years old.';
```

However, this method can become cumbersome when dealing with multiple strings. Template literals (also known as template strings) provide a cleaner and more concise way to concatenate strings.

Example:

```
const greeting = `Hello, my name is ${name} and I am ${age} years old.`;
```

Template literals use backticks (`) instead of quotes. Inside the backticks, we can use `${}` to embed JavaScript expressions, including variables and calculations.

String Properties and Methods

Strings in JavaScript have various properties and methods that allow us to manipulate and interact with them.

Example:

```
const s = 'Hello world';

// Get the length of the string
const length = s.length; // 11
```

```javascript
// Convert the string to uppercase
const upper = s.toUpperCase(); // 'HELLO WORLD'
```

Properties are attributes of the string, while methods are functions that can be performed on the string. When using properties, we do not use parentheses, but we do use parentheses for methods.

Behind the scenes, JavaScript creates a string object when we use properties or methods on a string. This allows us to access the string's properties and methods even though strings are primitive values.

Accessing Individual Characters and Prototype

Strings in JavaScript can be accessed by their individual characters using the [ ] syntax. The index starts at 0, just like an array.

Example:

```javascript
const s = 'Hello world';

// Get the first character
const firstChar = s[0]; // 'H'

// Get the second character
const secondChar = s[1]; // 'e'
```

Objects in JavaScript have a prototype, which is where their methods are stored. We can access the prototype using the __proto__ property.

Example:

```javascript
const s = 'Hello world';

// Access the prototype
const prototype = s.__proto__;

// Log the prototype
console.log(prototype);
```

This will log the prototype object, which contains all the methods available for strings.

String Properties and Methods

- **toUpperCase()**: Converts the string to uppercase.
- **toLowerCase()**: Converts the string to lowercase.
- **charAt(index)**: Returns the character at the specified index.
- **indexOf(value)**: Returns the index of the first occurrence of the specified value.
- **substring(start, end)**: Returns a substring from the start index to the end index (excluding the end index).

Example:

```javascript
const s = 'Hello world';

// Convert to uppercase
const upper = s.toUpperCase(); // 'HELLO WORLD'

// Get the index of 'e'
const indexOfE = s.indexOf('e'); // 1

// Get a substring from index 0 to 4
const substring = s.substring(0, 4); // 'Hell'
```

Substring and Slice

- **substring(start, end)**: Returns a substring from the start index to the end index (excluding the end index).
- **slice(start, end)**: Similar to `substring`, but can also start from the end using negative numbers.

Example:

```javascript
const s = 'Hello world';

// Get a substring from index 0 to 4
const substring = s.substring(0, 4); // 'Hell'
```

```javascript
// Get a substring from index 2 to 5
const slice = s.slice(2, 5); // 'llo'

// Get a substring from the end of the string
const sliceFromEnd = s.slice(-4); // 'orld'
```

Trim

- **trim()**: Removes whitespace from the beginning and end of a string.

Example:

```javascript
const s = '   Hello world   ';

// Trim the whitespace
const trimmed = s.trim(); // 'Hello world'
```

Replace

- **replace(searchValue, replaceValue)**: Replaces all occurrences of a specified value with another value.

Example:

```javascript
const s = 'Hello world';

// Replace 'world' with 'John'
const replaced = s.replace('world', 'John'); // 'Hello John'
```

Includes

- **includes(searchValue)**: Returns `true` if the specified value is found within the string, otherwise returns `false`.

Example:

```javascript
const s = 'Hello world';

// Check if 'world' is included in the string
const includesWorld = s.includes('world'); // true
```

valueOf()

- **valueOf()**: Returns the primitive value of a variable.

Example:

```
const s = 'Hello world';

// Get the primitive value of the string
const primitiveValue = s.valueOf(); // 'Hello world'
```

Split

- **split(separator)**: Splits a string into an array based on a specified separator.

Example:

```
const s = 'Hello world';

// Split the string by the space character
const splitBySpace = s.split(' '); // ['Hello', 'world']

// Split the string into individual characters
const splitByCharacter = s.split(''); // ['H', 'e', 'l', 'l', 'o', ' ', 'w', 'o', 'r', 'l', 'd']
```

Challenge: Capitalize

Task: Write a function that takes a string with a single word and capitalizes the first letter.

Example:

```
capitalize('developer'); // 'Developer'
```

Hints:

- Use the `charAt()` method to get the character at a specific index.
- Use bracket notation (e.g., `myString[0]`) to access the first character.
- Use `toUpperCase()` to convert a character to uppercase.

String : 39

- Use substring() or slice() to extract a substring from the string.

Solution 1:
```
const string = 'challenge'
// Get the first character and convert it to uppercase
const firstCharacter = string.charAt(0).toUpperCase();

// Get the rest of the string
const restOfString = string.substring(1);

// Concatenate the uppercase first character with the rest of the string
console.log(firstCharacter + restOfString);
```

Solution 2:
```
const string = 'challenge'
// Get the first character and convert it to uppercase
const firstCharacter = string[0].toUpperCase();

// Get the rest of the string
const restOfString = string.substring(1);

// Concatenate the uppercase first character with the rest of the string
console.log(firstCharacter + restOfString);
}
```

Solution 3:
```
const string = 'challenge'
// Get the first character and convert it to uppercase
const firstCharacter = string.charAt(0).toUpperCase();

// Get the rest of the string
const restOfString = string.slice(1);

// Use template literals to concatenate the uppercase first character with the rest of the string
console.log(`${firstCharacter}${restOfString}`);
```

Number

Number Objects

Just like strings, numbers have methods and properties that can be used to manipulate and interact with them. We can create a number object using the `Number` constructor:

```
const num = new Number(5);
```

However, it's more common to use the primitive number type directly:

```
const num = 5;
```

Converting Numbers to Strings

To convert a number to a string, we can use the `toString()` method:

```
const numString = num.toString();
```

Getting the Length of a Number

Numbers do not have a `length` property. However, we can get the number of digits in a number by converting it to a string and then using the `length` property of the string:

```
const numLength = numString.length;
```

Formatting Numbers with `toFixed()`

The `toFixed()` method allows us to specify the number of decimal places to display in a number:

```
const formattedNum = num.toFixed(2); // "5.00"
```

Example:

```
const num = 5.4567;
const numString = num.toString();
```

```javascript
const numLength = numString.length;
const formattedNum = num.toFixed(2);

console.log(numString);    // "5.4567"
console.log(numLength);    // 6
console.log(formattedNum); // "5.46"
```

toFixed() vs. toPrecision()

toFixed() rounds the number to the specified number of decimal places, while toPrecision() rounds the number to the specified number of significant digits.

```javascript
const num = 5.4567;
const fixedNum = num.toFixed(2);       // "5.46"
const precisionNum = num.toPrecision(2); // "5.5"
```

toExponential()

The toExponential() method converts a number to exponential notation. The first argument specifies the number of digits to display after the decimal point.

```javascript
const num = 9.9;
const exponentialNum = num.toExponential(2); // "9.90e+0"
```

toLocaleString()

The toLocaleString() method formats a number according to the locale specified in the first argument.

```javascript
const num = 5;
const localeNum = num.toLocaleString('ar-EG'); // "٥"
```

Number Properties

Number.MAX_VALUE

This property represents the largest possible number that can be represented in JavaScript.

```javascript
const maxValue = Number.MAX_VALUE; // 1.7976931348623157e+308
```

Number.MIN_VALUE

This property represents the smallest possible number that can be represented in JavaScript.

```javascript
const minValue = Number.MIN_VALUE; // 5e-324
```

Number.NaN

This property represents the "Not-a-Number" value.

```javascript
const nan = Number.NaN;
```

Math Methods

Math.abs()

The Math.abs() method returns the absolute value of a number.

```javascript
const num = -5;
const absoluteNum = Math.abs(num); // 5
```

Math.round()

The Math.round() method rounds a number to the nearest integer.

```javascript
const num = 4.6;
const roundedNum = Math.round(num); // 5
```

Math.ceil()

The Math.ceil() method rounds a number up to the nearest integer.

```javascript
const num = 4.2;
const ceilNum = Math.ceil(num); // 5
```

Math.floor()

The Math.floor() method rounds a number down to the nearest integer.

```
const num = 4.9;
const floorNum = Math.floor(num); // 4
```

Math.pow()

The `Math.pow()` method returns the value of a number raised to a specified power.

```
const num = 2;
const powNum = Math.pow(num, 3); // 8
```

Math.min() and Math.max()

The `Math.min()` and `Math.max()` methods return the smallest and largest of two or more numbers, respectively.

```
const num1 = 4;
const num2 = 5;
const minNum = Math.min(num1, num2); // 4
const maxNum = Math.max(num1, num2); // 5
```

Math.random()

The `Math.random()` method returns a random decimal number between 0 and 1.

```
const randomNum = Math.random(); // 0.123456789
```

To generate a random integer between a specified range, you can use the following formula:

```
const min = 1;
const max = 10;
const randomInt = Math.floor(Math.random() * (max - min + 1)) + min;
```

Challenge: Random Number Operations

Create a variable called x that is a random number between 1 and 100, and a variable called y that is a random number between 1 and 50. Then, create variables for the sum, difference, product, quotient, and remainder of x and y. Finally, log the output in a string that shows the two numbers of x and y along with the operator and result.

Hints:

- The `Math.random()` function returns a floating-point pseudo-random number in the range of 0 to less than 1.
- The `Math.floor()` function will round a number down to the nearest integer.

Example:

```
const x = Math.floor(Math.random() * 100) + 1;
const y = Math.floor(Math.random() * 50) + 1;

const sum = x + y;
const difference = x - y;
const product = x * y;
const quotient = x / y;
const remainder = x % y;

console.log(`${x} + ${y} = ${sum}`);
console.log(`${x} - ${y} = ${difference}`);
console.log(`${x} * ${y} = ${product}`);
console.log(`${x} / ${y} = ${quotient}`);
console.log(`${x} % ${y} = ${remainder}`);
```

Output:

```
31 + 15 = 46
31 - 15 = 16
31 * 15 = 465
31 / 15 = 2.0666666666666666
31 % 15 = 1
```

The output will vary depending on the random numbers generated for x and y.

Dates and Times

Dates and times are important in programming, and JavaScript has a `Date` object that represents a point in time and allows you to perform basic operations on it.

Creating a Date Object

To create a new `Date` object, use the `new` keyword:

```
const d = new Date();
console.log(d); // Output: Fri Oct 28 2022 16:30:39 GMT-0700 (Pacific Daylight Time)
```

Converting to a String

You can convert a `Date` object to a string using the `toString()` method:

```
console.log(d.toString()); // Output: Fri Oct 28 2022 16:30:39 GMT-0700 (Pacific Daylight Time)
```

Setting a Specific Date

To set a specific date, pass arguments to the `Date` constructor:

```
const d = new Date(2021, 6, 10); // July 10, 2021
console.log(d); // Output: Sat Jul 10 2021 00:00:00 GMT-0700 (Pacific Daylight Time)
```

Months in JavaScript are zero-indexed, so July is represented by the number 6.

Setting a Specific Time

To set a specific time, add additional arguments to the `Date` constructor:

```
const d = new Date(2021, 6, 10, 12, 30, 0); // July 10, 2021, 12:30 PM
```

```
console.log(d); // Output: Sat Jul 10 2021 12:30:00 GMT-0700
(Pacific Daylight Time)
```

Setting a Date and Time Using a String

You can also set a date and time using a string in a specific format:

```
const d = new Date("2021-07-10T12:30:00"); // July 10, 2021,
12:30 PM
console.log(d); // Output: Sat Jul 10 2021 12:30:00 GMT-0700
(Pacific Daylight Time)
```

When using hyphens in the date string, the year must come after the month for accurate results.

Timestamps

A Unix timestamp is an integer representing the number of milliseconds that have elapsed since January 1, 1970. In JavaScript, timestamps are expressed in milliseconds.

Getting a Timestamp

To get the current timestamp, use `Date.now()`:

```
const timestamp = Date.now();
console.log(timestamp); // Output: 1667011200000 (example
value)
```

Getting a Timestamp for a Specific Date

To get the timestamp for a specific date, use the `getTime()` method on a Date object:

```
const d = new Date(2022, 7, 10, 12, 30, 0); // July 10, 2022,
12:30 PM
const timestamp = d.getTime();
console.log(timestamp); // Output: 1657429400000
```

Creating a Date Object from a Timestamp

To create a `Date` object from a timestamp, use the `new Date()` constructor:

```
const d = new Date(timestamp);
console.log(d); // Output: Sun Jul 10 2022 12:30:00 GMT-0700 (Pacific Daylight Time)
```

Converting Timestamps to Seconds

To convert a timestamp from milliseconds to seconds, divide it by 1000:

```
const seconds = Math.floor(timestamp / 1000);
console.log(seconds); // Output: 1657429400 (example value)
```

Getting Specific Date Parts

To get specific parts of a date, use the following methods on the `Date` object:

- `getFullYear()`: Returns the year as a four-digit number.
- `getMonth()`: Returns the month as a zero-based index (0-11).
- `getDate()`: Returns the day of the month as a number (1-31).
- `getDay()`: Returns the day of the week as a number (0-6, where 0 is Sunday).

Example:

```
const d = new Date();

console.log(d.getFullYear()); // Output: 2022
console.log(d.getMonth() + 1); // Output: 10 (October, zero-based)
console.log(d.getDate()); // Output: 28
console.log(d.getDay()); // Output: 5 (Friday)
```

Getting Specific Time Parts

To get specific time parts, use the following methods on the `Date` object:

- `getHours()`: Returns the hour (0-23).
- `getMinutes()`: Returns the minutes (0-59).
- `getSeconds()`: Returns the seconds (0-59).
- `getMilliseconds()`: Returns the milliseconds (0-999).

Example:

```
const d = new Date();

console.log(d.getHours()); // Output: 9
console.log(d.getMinutes()); // Output: 37
console.log(d.getSeconds()); // Output: 23
console.log(d.getMilliseconds()); // Output: 123
```

Creating Dates from Specific Parts

You can also create a `Date` object from specific parts using template literals:

```
const d = new Date(`${d.getFullYear()}-${d.getMonth() + 1}-${d.getDate()} ${d.getHours()}:${d.getMinutes()}:${d.getSeconds()}`);
```

Formatting Dates with `Intl.DateTimeFormat`

The `Intl.DateTimeFormat` API provides a more modern and powerful way to format dates in a locale-sensitive way. It allows you to specify the locale (e.g., "en-US" for the United States) and pass in options to customize the format.

Example:

```
const d = new Date();

// Format the date as a string using the default locale
const x = Intl.DateTimeFormat().format(d);
console.log(x); // Output: "10/28/22"

// Format the date as a string using a specific locale
```

```javascript
const y = Intl.DateTimeFormat("en-GB").format(d);
console.log(y); // Output: "28/10/22" (day-first format)

// Format the date as a string using options
const z = Intl.DateTimeFormat("default", {
  month: "long",
}).format(d);
console.log(z); // Output: "October"
```

Shorter Syntax Using `toLocaleString()`

You can also use the `toLocaleString()` method on the `Date` object to format the date using the `Intl.DateTimeFormat` API. This provides a shorter syntax:

```javascript
const d = new Date();

// Format the date as a string using the default locale and
options
const x = d.toLocaleString("default", {
  weekday: "long",
  month: "long",
  year: "numeric",
  hour: "numeric",
  minute: "numeric",
  timeZone: "America/New_York",
});
console.log(x); // Output: "Friday, October 28, 2022 at 6:49:11 AM"
```

This method allows you to easily customize the format of the date without having to call the `Intl.DateTimeFormat` API directly.

Arrays

Arrays are a special type of object in JavaScript that can store multiple values. They are created using square brackets ([ ]) and the values within the array are called elements.

Creating Arrays

There are two ways to create an array in JavaScript:

- **Array literal:** This is the most common way to create an array. Simply enclose the elements in square brackets:

```javascript
const numbers = [1, 2, 3, 4, 5];
const fruits = ["apple", "grape", "orange"];
```

- **Array constructor:** You can also use the Array constructor to create an array:

```javascript
const fruits = new Array("apple", "grape", "orange");
```

Accessing Array Elements

To access a specific element in an array, use the index of the element. Arrays are zero-based, meaning the first element has an index of 0.

```javascript
const firstNumber = numbers[0]; // 1
const lastFruit = fruits[fruits.length - 1]; // "orange"
```

Example:

```javascript
const numbers = [1, 2, 3, 4, 5];

// Access the first element
const firstNumber = numbers[0];
console.log(firstNumber); // Output: 1

// Access the last element
```

```javascript
const lastNumber = numbers[numbers.length - 1];
console.log(lastNumber); // Output: 5
```

Manipulating Arrays

Arrays in JavaScript are mutable, meaning you can change their contents.

Accessing and Changing Elements

To access an element in an array, use the index of the element. To change an element, simply assign a new value to the index.

```javascript
const fruits = ["apple", "grape", "orange"];

// Access the second element
const secondFruit = fruits[1]; // "grape"

// Change the second element
fruits[1] = "pear";

console.log(fruits); // ["apple", "pear", "orange"]
```

Adding Elements

To add an element to the end of an array, you can use the `push()` method.

```javascript
fruits.push("banana");

console.log(fruits); // ["apple", "pear", "orange", "banana"]
```

You can also use the `unshift()` method to add an element to the beginning of an array.

```javascript
fruits.unshift("strawberry");

console.log(fruits); // ["strawberry", "apple", "pear", "orange", "banana"]
```

Removing Elements

To remove an element from the end of an array, you can use the `pop()` method.

```
const lastFruit = fruits.pop(); // "banana"

console.log(fruits); // ["strawberry", "apple", "pear", "orange"]
```

You can also use the `shift()` method to remove an element from the beginning of an array.

```
const firstFruit = fruits.shift(); // "strawberry"

console.log(fruits); // ["apple", "pear", "orange"]
```

Getting the Length

The `length` property of an array returns the number of elements in the array.

```
const length = fruits.length; // 3
```

Example:

```
const fruits = ["apple", "grape", "orange"];

// Add "banana" to the end of the array
fruits.push("banana");

// Remove "grape" from the array
fruits.splice(1, 1);

// Get the length of the array
const length = fruits.length;

console.log(fruits); // ["apple", "orange", "banana"]
console.log(length); // 3
```

Array Methods

In addition to accessing and changing elements by index, arrays in JavaScript have a number of built-in methods that allow you to manipulate and get information from them.

Mutating Methods

- **push()**: Adds an element to the end of the array.
- **pop()**: Removes the last element from the array and returns it.
- **unshift()**: Adds an element to the beginning of the array.
- **shift()**: Removes the first element from the array and returns it.
- **reverse()**: Reverses the order of the elements in the array.

Example:

```javascript
const numbers = [1, 2, 3, 4, 5];

// Add 6 to the end of the array
numbers.push(6);

// Remove the last element from the array
const lastNumber = numbers.pop();

// Add 0 to the beginning of the array
numbers.unshift(0);

// Remove the first element from the array
const firstNumber = numbers.shift();

// Reverse the order of the elements in the array
numbers.reverse();

console.log(numbers); // [5, 4, 3, 2, 1, 0]
```

Non-Mutating Methods

- **includes()**: Checks if the array contains a specific value and returns a boolean.

- **indexOf()**: Returns the index of the first occurrence of a specific value in the array, or -1 if the value is not found.

Example:

```
const fruits = ["apple", "orange", "banana"];

// Check if the array contains "apple"
const hasApple = fruits.includes("apple"); // true

// Get the index of the first occurrence of "banana"
const bananaIndex = fruits.indexOf("banana"); // 2
```

The mutating methods (push(), pop(), unshift(), shift(), and reverse()) change the original array, while the non-mutating methods (includes() and indexOf()) do not.

indexOf() and slice()

The indexOf() method returns the index of the first occurrence of a specific value in an array, or -1 if the value is not found.

Example:

```
const fruits = ["apple", "orange", "banana"];

// Get the index of the first occurrence of "banana"
const bananaIndex = fruits.indexOf("banana"); // 2
```

The slice() method returns a new array containing a portion of the original array. The first argument specifies the start index, and the second argument (optional) specifies the end index.

Example:

```
const numbers = [1, 2, 3, 4, 5];

// Get a new array containing the elements from index 1 to 3
const subarray = numbers.slice(1, 3); // [2, 3]
```

splice()

The `splice()` method modifies the original array by removing or replacing elements. It takes three arguments:

- **Start index:** The index at which to start removing or replacing elements.
- **Delete count:** The number of elements to remove.
- **Items to add:** (Optional) The elements to add to the array at the specified index.

Example:

```javascript
const fruits = ["apple", "orange", "banana", "cherry"];

// Remove the element at index 1 (orange)
fruits.splice(1, 1); // ["apple", "banana", "cherry"]

// Replace the element at index 2 (banana) with "strawberry"
fruits.splice(2, 1, "strawberry"); // ["apple", "banana", "strawberry", "cherry"]

// Add "kiwi" to the end of the array
fruits.splice(fruits.length, 0, "kiwi"); // ["apple", "banana", "strawberry", "cherry", "kiwi"]
```

Note:

- `slice()` returns a new array, while `splice()` modifies the original array.
- `splice()` can be used to both remove and add elements, while `slice()` can only be used to extract elements.

Methods in JavaScript can be chained together to perform multiple operations on a single object.

Example:

```javascript
const fruits = ["apple", "orange", "banana", "cherry"];

// Get a new array containing the elements from index 1 to 3,
// reversed, and converted to a string
const result = fruits
  .slice(1, 3) // ["orange", "banana"]
  .reverse() // ["banana", "orange"]
  .join(", "); // "banana, orange"
```

Nesting Arrays

Arrays can contain other arrays, creating a nested structure.

Example:

```javascript
const fruits = ["apple", "orange"];
const berries = ["strawberry", "blueberry", "raspberry"];

// Create a nested array containing the fruits and berries
arrays
const fruitsAndBerries = [fruits, berries];

// Access the first element of the nested array (the fruits
array)
const firstFruit = fruitsAndBerries[0][0]; // "apple"
```

Concatenating Arrays

The concat() method can be used to combine multiple arrays into a single array.

Example:

```javascript
const fruits = ["apple", "orange"];
const berries = ["strawberry", "blueberry", "raspberry"];

// Concatenate the fruits and berries arrays
const fruitsAndBerries = fruits.concat(berries); // ["apple",
"orange", "strawberry", "blueberry", "raspberry"]
```

Spread Operator

The spread operator (...) can be used to spread the elements of an array into another array or object.

Example:

```
const fruits = ["apple", "orange"];
const berries = ["strawberry", "blueberry", "raspberry"];

// Spread the elements of the fruits array into a new array
const newFruits = [...fruits]; // ["apple", "orange"]

// Spread the elements of the fruits and berries arrays into a new array
const fruitsAndBerries = [...fruits, ...berries]; // ["apple", "orange", "strawberry", "blueberry", "raspberry"]
```

Spread Operator vs. `concat()`

The spread operator and the `concat()` method can both be used to combine arrays. However, there are some key differences between the two:

- The spread operator creates a new array, while `concat()` modifies the original array.
- The spread operator can be used to spread the elements of an array into another array or object, while `concat()` can only be used to combine arrays.

Example:

```
const fruits = ["apple", "orange"];
const berries = ["strawberry", "blueberry", "raspberry"];

// Spread the elements of the fruits and berries arrays into a new array
const fruitsAndBerries = [...fruits, ...berries]; // ["apple", "orange", "strawberry", "blueberry", "raspberry"]
```

```javascript
// Concatenate the fruits and berries arrays
const fruitsAndBerries2 = fruits.concat(berries); //
["apple", "orange", "strawberry", "blueberry", "raspberry"]
```

Flattening Arrays

The `flat()` method can be used to flatten a nested array into a single-level array.

Example:

```javascript
const nestedArray = [1, 2, [3, 4], [5, 6, [7, 8]]];

// Flatten the nested array
const flattenedArray = nestedArray.flat(); // [1, 2, 3, 4, 5, 6, 7, 8]
```

Static Methods on the Array Object

The `Array` object has several static methods that can be used to create and manipulate arrays.

- `Array.isArray()`: Checks if a value is an array.
- `Array.from()`: Creates an array from an array-like object (e.g., a string, HTML collection, etc.).
- `Array.of()`: Creates an array from a set of values.

Example:

```javascript
// Check if a value is an array
const isArray = Array.isArray([1, 2, 3]); // true

// Create an array from a string
const arrayFromString = Array.from("12345"); // ["1", "2", "3", "4", "5"]

// Create an array from a set of values
const arrayFromValues = Array.of(1, 2, 3); // [1, 2, 3]
```

Array Challenges

Challenge 1

Create an array with numbers 1 through 5, and then mutate it using array methods to turn it into an array with numbers 6 through 0.

Solution:

```javascript
const array = [1, 2, 3, 4, 5];

// Reverse the array
array.reverse();

// Push 0 onto the end of the array
array.push(0);

// Unshift 6 onto the beginning of the array
array.unshift(6);

console.log(array); // [6, 5, 4, 3, 2, 1, 0]
```

Challenge 2

Combine array one and array two, but have the result not have the extra 5.

Solution 1:

```javascript
const arrayOne = [1, 2, 3, 4, 5];
const arrayTwo = [5, 6, 7, 8, 9, 10];

// Concatenate the arrays
const combinedArray = arrayOne.concat(arrayTwo);

// Remove the extra 5 using the slice() method
const result = combinedArray.slice(0, 10);

console.log(result); // [1, 2, 3, 4, 5, 6, 7, 8, 9, 10]
```

Solution 2:

```javascript
const arrayOne = [1, 2, 3, 4, 5];
const arrayTwo = [5, 6, 7, 8, 9, 10];

// Spread the arrays into a new array
const combinedArray = [...arrayOne, ...arrayTwo];

// Use the filter() method to remove the extra 5
const result = combinedArray.filter(element => element !== 5);

console.log(result); // [1, 2, 3, 4, 6, 7, 8, 9, 10]
```

Solution 3:

```javascript
const arrayOne = [1, 2, 3, 4, 5];
const arrayTwo = [5, 6, 7, 8, 9, 10];

// Concatenate array one and array two using the spread operator
const combinedArray = [...arrayOne, ...arrayTwo];

// Splice the extra 5 from the combined array
combinedArray.splice(4, 1);

console.log(combinedArray); // [1, 2, 3, 4, 6, 7, 8, 9, 10]
```

Object Literals

Object literals are key-value pairs enclosed in curly braces. Each key is a string, and each value can be any data type.

```
const person = {
  name: "John Doe",
  age: 30,
  isMarried: true
};
```

In the example above, "name", "age", and "isMarried" are the keys, and "John Doe", 30, and true are the values.

Object literals can be used to store and organize data in a structured way. They are commonly used to represent real-world objects, such as users, products, or orders.

Accessing and Modifying Object Properties

To access a specific property from an object, use the dot syntax:

```
const person = {
  name: "John Doe",
  age: 30,
  isAdmin: true
};

console.log(person.name); // "John Doe"
```

You can also use bracket notation, which is useful when the property name is stored in a variable:

```
const propertyName = "age";
console.log(person[propertyName]); // 30
```

To update a property, simply assign a new value to it:

```js
person.name = "Jane Doe";
console.log(person.name); // "Jane Doe"
```

To add a new property, use the dot or bracket notation:

```js
person.hasChildren = true;
console.log(person.hasChildren); // true
```

To delete a property, use the `delete` operator:

```js
delete person.age;
console.log(person.age); // undefined
```

Nested Objects and Arrays

Objects can contain other objects and arrays as properties:

```js
const person = {
  name: "John Doe",
  address: {
    street: "123 Main Street",
    city: "Boston",
    state: "MA"
  },
  hobbies: ["music", "sports"]
};

console.log(person.address.state); // "MA"
console.log(person.hobbies[0]); // "music"
```

Functions as Object Properties

Functions can also be added as properties to objects:

```js
const person = {
  name: "John Doe",
  greet: function() {
    console.log("Hello, my name is " + this.name);
  }
};
```

```
person.greet(); // "Hello, my name is John Doe"
```

Note that the `this` keyword inside the function refers to the object itself.

Object Keys with Multiple Words

While it's not recommended, you can use multiple words in object keys by surrounding them with quotes:

```
const person = {
  "first name": "Brad",
  "last name": "Pitt"
};

console.log(person["first name"]); // "Brad"
```

However, it's better to use camelCase or snake_case for object keys.

Spread Operator with Objects

The spread operator can also be used with objects to create a new object with the properties of the original object:

```
const person1 = {
  name: "John Doe",
  age: 30
};

const person2 = {
  ...person1,
  isAdmin: true
};

console.log(person2); // { name: "John Doe", age: 30, isAdmin: true }
```

The spread operator can be used to combine multiple objects into a new object:

Object Literals

```javascript
const obj1 = { a: 1, b: 2 };
const obj2 = { c: 3, d: 4 };

const obj3 = { ...obj1, ...obj2 };
console.log(obj3); // { a: 1, b: 2, c: 3, d: 4 }
```

Object Constructor

Objects can also be created using the `Object` constructor:

```javascript
const todo = new Object();
todo.id = 1;
todo.name = "Buy milk";
todo.completed = false;

console.log(todo); // { id: 1, name: "Buy milk", completed: false }
```

This is equivalent to using an object literal:

```javascript
const todo = {
  id: 1,
  name: "Buy milk",
  completed: false
};
```

Custom Constructors

We can create our own custom constructors for objects:

```javascript
function ToDo(id, name, completed) {
  this.id = id;
  this.name = name;
  this.completed = completed;
}

const todo1 = new ToDo(1, "Buy milk", false);
console.log(todo1); // ToDo { id: 1, name: "Buy milk", completed: false }
```

Nesting Objects

Objects can be nested within other objects:

```
const person = {
  name: "John Doe",
  address: {
    coordinates: {
      latitude: 42.1234,
      longitude: -71.5678
    }
  }
};

console.log(person.address.coordinates.latitude); // 42.1234
```

Object.assign()

The `Object.assign()` method can also be used to combine multiple objects into a new object:

```
const obj4 = Object.assign({}, obj1, obj2);
console.log(obj4); // { a: 1, b: 2, c: 3, d: 4 }
```

Note that `Object.assign()` modifies the first argument passed in, so it's better to use the spread operator if you don't want to modify the original objects.

Arrays of Objects

We often deal with arrays of objects, such as to-do lists or user profiles. For example:

```
const todos = [
  { id: 1, name: "Buy milk", completed: false },
  { id: 2, name: "Pick up kids from school", completed: false },
  { id: 3, name: "Take out trash", completed: false }
];
```

Accessing Object Properties

To access a specific property of an object in an array, use bracket syntax:

```
console.log(todos[0].name); // "Buy milk"
```

Object.keys()

The `Object.keys()` method returns an array of the keys in an object:

```
const keys = Object.keys(todos[0]);
console.log(keys); // ["id", "name", "completed"]
```

Object.values()

The `Object.values()` method returns an array of the values in an object:

```
const values = Object.values(todos[0]);
console.log(values); // [1, "Buy milk", false]
```

Object.entries()

The `Object.entries()` method returns an array of key-value pairs in an object:

```
const entries = Object.entries(todos[0]);
console.log(entries); // [["id", 1], ["name", "Buy milk"],
["completed", false]]
```

Object.entries() and Object.hasOwnProperty()

The `Object.entries()` method returns an array of key-value pairs in an object:

```
const entries = Object.entries(todos[0]);
console.log(entries); // [["id", 1], ["name", "Buy milk"],
["completed", false]]
```

The `Object.hasOwnProperty()` method returns a Boolean indicating if the object has a specific property:

```
console.log(todos[0].hasOwnProperty("name")); // true
console.log(todos[0].hasOwnProperty("age")); // false
```

Shorthand Object Properties

When creating an object, if the key and value are the same, you can use shorthand notation:

```
const person = {
  firstName,
  lastName,
  age
};
```

This is equivalent to:

```
const person = {
  firstName: firstName,
  lastName: lastName,
  age: age
};
```

Destructuring

Destructuring allows you to extract properties from an object into variables:

```
const { id, title } = todo;
console.log(id); // 1
console.log(title); // "Take out trash"
```

This is equivalent to:

```
const id = todo.id;
const title = todo.title;
```

Destructuring Nested Objects and Arrays

You can destructure nested objects by using multiple levels of curly braces:

```javascript
const { user: { name } } = todo;
console.log(name); // "John Doe"
```

You can rename properties when destructuring by using a colon:

```javascript
const { id: todoId } = todo;
console.log(todoId); // 1
```

Destructuring Arrays

You can destructure arrays using square brackets:

```javascript
const [first, second] = numbers;
console.log(first); // 23
console.log(second); // 67
```

You can use the rest operator (...) to collect the remaining elements of an array into a variable:

```javascript
const [first, second, ...rest] = numbers;
console.log(rest); // [33, 49, 52]
```

JSON (JavaScript Object Notation)

JSON (JavaScript Object Notation) is a lightweight data interchange format that is similar to JavaScript object literals. It is often used to send and receive data from servers in web development.

JSON data is typically stored in a string, with keys enclosed in double quotes and values enclosed in double quotes (for strings) or left unquoted (for numbers).

For example, the following JSON string represents an array of two objects:

```
[
  {
    "id": 1,
    "title": "Take out trash"
  },
```

```
  {
    "id": 2,
    "title": "Do laundry"
  }
]
```

You can use the `JSON.parse()` method to convert a JSON string into a JavaScript object:

```
const data = JSON.parse('[{"id": 1, "title": "Take out trash"}, {"id": 2, "title": "Do laundry"}]');
console.log(data); // [{id: 1, title: "Take out trash"}, {id: 2, title: "Do Laundry"}]
```

You can also use the `JSON.stringify()` method to convert a JavaScript object into a JSON string:

```
const data = {
  id: 1,
  title: "Take out trash"
};
const json = JSON.stringify(data);
console.log(json); // "{\"id\":1,\"title\":\"Take out trash\"}"
```

Converting JavaScript Objects to JSON

We can use the `JSON.stringify()` method to convert a JavaScript object into a JSON string:

```
const post = {
  id: 1,
  title: "Post One",
  body: "This is the body of the post."
};

const json = JSON.stringify(post);
console.log(json); // "{\"id\":1,\"title\":\"Post One\",\"body\":\"This is the body of the post.\"}"
```

We can use the `JSON.parse()` method to convert a JSON string back into a JavaScript object:

```
const obj = JSON.parse(json);
console.log(obj); // {id: 1, title: "Post One", body: "This
is the body of the post."}
```

Using JSON with Local Storage

Local storage is a way to store data on the client side in the browser. However, local storage can only store strings, so we need to convert our JavaScript objects to JSON strings before storing them in local storage.

To store a JavaScript object in local storage, we can use the following steps:

1. Convert the object to a JSON string using `JSON.stringify()`.
2. Store the JSON string in local storage using `localStorage.setItem()`.

To retrieve a JavaScript object from local storage, we can use the following steps:

1. Retrieve the JSON string from local storage using `localStorage.getItem()`.
2. Convert the JSON string back to a JavaScript object using `JSON.parse()`.

JSON Arrays

JSON can also represent arrays of objects. For example, the following JSON string represents an array of two objects:

```
[
  {
    "id": 1,
    "title": "Post One"
  },
  {
    "id": 2,
```

```
    "title": "Post Two"
  }
]
```

We can convert a JavaScript array of objects to a JSON string using `JSON.stringify()`, and we can convert a JSON string representing an array of objects back to a JavaScript array using `JSON.parse()`.

Accessing JSON Properties

To access a property of a JSON object, we can use the dot notation or the bracket notation. For example, the following code accesses the `id` property of the first object in the `posts` array:

```
const posts = JSON.parse('[{"id": 1, "title": "Post One"}, {"id": 2, "title": "Post Two"}]');
console.log(posts[0].id); // 1
```

It is important to remember that we cannot access the properties of a JSON string directly. We must first parse the JSON string into a JavaScript object before we can access its properties.

Object Challenge

Create an Array of Objects

Create an array of objects called `library` with three objects inside. Each object should have the following properties:

- `title` (string)
- `author` (string)
- `status` (object with the following properties):
    - `own` (boolean)
    - `reading` (boolean)
    - `read` (boolean)

Set `own` to `true` for all objects, and set `reading` and `read` to `false`.

Example:

```
const library = [
  {
    title: "The Road Ahead",
    author: "Bill Gates",
    status: {
      own: true,
      reading: false,
      read: false
    }
  },
  {
    title: "Steve Jobs",
    author: "Walter Isaacson",
    status: {
      own: true,
      reading: false,
      read: false
    }
  },
  {
    title: "Mockingjay",
    author: "Suzanne Collins",
    status: {
      own: true,
      reading: false,
      read: false
    }
  }
];
```

Set the read Value to True for All Books

Set the read value to true for all books in the `library` array. Do not edit the initial objects; instead, use dot notation to modify the values.

Example:

```
library[0].status.read = true;
library[1].status.read = true;
library[2].status.read = true;
```

Destructure the Title from the First Book

Destructure the `title` property from the first book in the `library` array and rename the variable to `firstBook`.

Example:

```
const { title: firstBook } = library[0];
```

Destructure the Title from the First Book

To destructure the `title` property from the first book in the `library` array and rename the variable to `firstBook`, use the following syntax:

```
const { title: firstBook } = library[0];
```

This creates a new variable called `firstBook` that contains the `title` property of the first object in the `library` array.

Convert the Library Object to a JSON String

To convert the `library` object to a JSON string, use the following syntax:

```
const libraryJson = JSON.stringify(library);
```

This creates a new variable called `libraryJson` that contains the JSON representation of the `library` object.

Functions and Scope

Functions are blocks of code that can be executed multiple times. They can be used to group related code together and make it easier to read and understand.

There are several ways to create functions in JavaScript. One way is to use a function declaration:

```javascript
function myFunction() {
  // Code to be executed
}
```

Another way to create a function is to use a function expression:

```javascript
const myFunction = function() {
  // Code to be executed
};
```

Function scope refers to the visibility of variables and functions within a function. Variables and functions declared within a function are only accessible within that function.

Creating Functions

Functions are blocks of code that can be executed multiple times. They can be used to group related code together and make it easier to read and understand.

To create a function in JavaScript, you can use the `function` keyword followed by the function name and parentheses. The code that will be executed when the function is called goes inside the curly braces.

```javascript
function sayHello() {
   console.log("Hello world!");
}
```

Passing Data to Functions

When you call a function, you can pass data to it using parameters. Parameters are variables that are declared in the function definition.

```
function add(num1, num2) {
  console.log(num1 + num2);
}
```

When you call the add function, you pass in the arguments that will be assigned to the parameters.

```
add(5, 10); // Logs 15 to the console
```

Returning Values from Functions

The reason we return something from a function is because we want to do something with that value. For example, we can store the returned value in a variable.

```
const result = subtract(10, 2); // result will be 8
console.log(result); // Logs 8 to the console
```

We can also pass the returned value directly to another function.

```
console.log(subtract(20, 5)); // Logs 15 to the console
```

In some cases, we may not need to return a value from a function. For example, if we are sending a request to a backend or an API and updating something in a database, we might not need to return anything.

Arguments and Parameters

When we call a function, we can pass data to it using arguments. Arguments are the values that are passed to the function when it is called.

When we define a function, we can specify the parameters that the function will accept. Parameters are the variables that will hold the values passed to the function.

For example, the following function takes a single parameter called `user`:

```
function registerUser(user) {
  return user + " is registered";
}
```

When we call the `registerUser` function, we pass an argument to it:

```
const registeredUser = registerUser("John");
console.log(registeredUser); // Logs "John is registered" to the console
```

Default Parameters

In JavaScript, we can specify default values for parameters. This means that if an argument is not passed to the function, the default value will be used.

There are two ways to specify default parameters:

- **Old way (pre-ES2015):** Use an `if` statement to check if the parameter is undefined and assign a default value if it is.
- **New way (ES2015+):** Use the = operator to assign a default value to the parameter in the function definition.

For example, the following function uses the new way to specify a default parameter:

```
function registerUser(user = "bot") {
  return user + " is registered";
}
```

If we call the `registerUser` function without passing an argument, the default value of "bot" will be used:

```
const registeredUser = registerUser();
console.log(registeredUser); // Logs "bot is registered" to the console
```

Rest Parameters

Rest parameters allow us to pass an arbitrary number of arguments to a function. The arguments are collected into an array, which can be accessed using the rest parameter.

For example, the following function takes a variable number of arguments and returns the sum of all the arguments:

```javascript
function sum(...numbers) {
  let total = 0;
  for (const num of numbers) {
    total += num;
  }
  return total;
}
```

We can call the `sum` function with any number of arguments, and it will always return the sum of all the arguments.

```javascript
console.log(sum(1, 2, 3)); // Logs 6 to the console
console.log(sum(1, 2, 3, 4, 5)); // Logs 15 to the console
```

Object Parameters

Functions can also accept objects as parameters. We can access the properties of the object using dot notation.

For example, the following function takes a user object as a parameter and returns a message with the user's name and ID:

```javascript
function loginUser(user) {
  return `User ${user.name} with ID ${user.id} is logged in`;
}
```

We can call the `loginUser` function with a user object as an argument:

```javascript
const user = {
  name: "John",
  id: 12345
};
```

```js
const message = loginUser(user);
console.log(message); // Logs "User John with ID 12345 is
logged in" to the console
```

Arrays as Parameters

Functions can also accept arrays as parameters. We can access the elements of the array using the index operator ([]).

For example, the following function takes an array of numbers as a parameter and returns a random number from the array:

```js
function getRandomNumber(array) {
  const randomIndex = Math.floor(Math.random() * array.length);
  const item = array[randomIndex];
  return item;
}
```

We can call the getRandomNumber function with an array of numbers as an argument:

```js
const numbers = [1, 2, 3, 4, 5, 6, 7, 8, 9, 10];
const randomNumber = getRandomNumber(numbers);
console.log(randomNumber); // Logs a random number from the
array to the console
```

Rest Parameters and Arrays

Rest parameters can also be used to pass an array of values to a function. The values are collected into an array, which can be accessed using the rest parameter.

For example, the following function takes a variable number of arguments and returns an array of the arguments:

```js
function getArgs(...args) {
  return args;
}
```

We can call the `getArgs` function with any number of arguments, and it will always return an array of the arguments:

```
console.log(getArgs(1, 2, 3)); // Logs [1, 2, 3] to the console
console.log(getArgs("John", "Sarah", "Bob")); // Logs ["John", "Sarah", "Bob"] to the console
```

Scope

Scope refers to the current area or context of a specific piece of code. There are two main types of scope in JavaScript:

- **Global scope:** Variables declared in the global scope are accessible from anywhere in the program.
- **Function scope:** Variables declared in a function are only accessible within that function.

Global Scope

Global scope refers to the variables and functions that are declared outside of any function or block. These variables and functions are accessible from anywhere in the program.

For example, the following code declares a global variable called `name`:

```
let name = "John";
```

This variable can be accessed from anywhere in the program, including within functions.

```
function sayHello() {
  console.log(`Hello, ${name}!`);
}

sayHello(); // Logs "Hello, John!" to the console
```

We can also access global variables and functions without using the `window` object. For example, we can simply call the `alert()` function without using `window.alert()`.

```
alert("Hello, world!"); // Displays an alert dialog with the
message "Hello, world!"
```

Function Scope

Function scope refers to the variables and functions that are declared within a function. These variables and functions are only accessible within that function.

For example, the following code declares a function-scoped variable called `message`:

```
function sayGoodbye() {
  let message = "Goodbye!";
  console.log(message); // Logs "Goodbye!" to the console
}

console.log(message); // Error: message is not defined
```

In this example, the `message` variable is only accessible within the `sayGoodbye()` function. Trying to access it outside of the function will result in an error.

Local Scope

Local scope refers to the scope of a variable or function within a specific block of code, such as a function or an if statement. Variables declared in a local scope are only accessible within that block of code.

For example, the following code declares a variable called `message` within an if statement:

```
if (true) {
  let message = "Hello, world!";
  console.log(message); // Logs "Hello, world!" to the console
}

console.log(message); // Error: message is not defined
```

In this example, the `message` variable is only accessible within the if statement. Trying to access it outside of the if statement will result in an error.

Block scope refers to the scope of a variable or function within a specific block of code, such as a function or an if statement. Variables declared in a block scope are only accessible within that block of code.

For example, the following code declares a variable called `message` within an if statement:

```
if (true) {
  let message = "Hello, world!";
  console.log(message); // Logs "Hello, world!" to the console
}

console.log(message); // Error: message is not defined
```

In this example, the `message` variable is only accessible within the if statement. Trying to access it outside of the if statement will result in an error.

Variable Shadowing

Variable shadowing occurs when a variable with the same name is declared in a nested scope. The inner variable takes precedence over the outer variable.

For example, the following code declares a global variable called x and a function-scoped variable also called x:

```
let x = 100;

function add() {
  const x = 50;

  const y = 100;
  console.log(x + y); // Logs 150 to the console
}
```

```
add();
```

In this example, the inner x variable shadows the outer x variable. When we call the add() function, the inner x variable is used, and the value of y is added to it.

VAR vs. LET and CONST

The var keyword is used to declare variables in JavaScript. However, var variables are not block-scoped. This means that they can be accessed from anywhere within the function or global scope in which they are declared.

For example, the following code declares a var variable called x in the global scope:

```
var x = 100;

function add() {
  var y = 50;
  console.log(x + y); // Logs 150 to the console
}

add();
```

In this example, the x variable is accessible from both the global scope and the add() function.

The let and const keywords were introduced in ES6 to address the limitations of var. let variables are block-scoped, meaning that they can only be accessed from within the block in which they are declared. const variables are also block-scoped, but they cannot be reassigned.

For example, the following code declares a let variable called message within an if statement:

```
if (true) {
  let message = "Hello, world!";
  console.log(message); // Logs "Hello, world!" to the
```

```
    console
}

console.log(message); // Error: message is not defined
```

In this example, the `message` variable is only accessible within the if statement. Trying to access it outside of the if statement will result in an error.

VAR is Function Scoped

The `var` keyword is function-scoped. This means that `var` variables can be accessed from anywhere within the function in which they are declared, even from within nested functions.

For example, the following code declares a `var` variable called d in the `run()` function:

```
function run() {
  var d = 100;
  console.log(d); // Logs 100 to the console
}

run();
```

In this example, the d variable is accessible from anywhere within the `run()` function, including from within the nested function `second()`.

```
function run() {
  var d = 100;

  function second() {
    console.log(d); // Logs 100 to the console
  }

  second();
}

run();
```

However, var variables declared in a function are not accessible from outside of that function.

```
function run() {
  var d = 100;
}

console.log(d); // Error: d is not defined
```

When a global variable is declared with var, it is added to the window object. This means that it can be accessed from anywhere in the global scope, even from within other functions.

For example, the following code declares a global variable called foo with var:

```
var foo = 1;

function bar() {
  console.log(foo); // Logs 1 to the console
}

bar();
```

In this example, the foo variable is accessible from within the bar() function because it is added to the window object.

Nested Functions and Nested Blocks

Nested functions and nested blocks create new scopes. This means that let or const variables declared in a nested function or block are only accessible within that function or block.

For example, the following code declares a nested function called second() within the first() function:

```
function first() {
  var x = 100;

  function second() {
```

```
    var y = 200;
    console.log(x + y); // Logs 300 to the console
  }

  second();
}

first();
```

In this example, the y variable is only accessible within the `second()` function. Trying to access it from outside of the function will result in an error.

```
function first() {
  var x = 100;

  function second() {
    var y = 200;
    console.log(x + y); // Logs 300 to the console
  }

  console.log(y); // Error: y is not defined
}

first();
```

Similarly, the following code declares a nested block within an if statement:

```
if (true) {
 const x = 100;

  if (x === 100) {
    const y = 200;

    var z = 200;
    console.log(x + y + z); // Logs 500 to the console
  }
}
```

```
console.log(y); // Error: y is not defined
console.log(z); // Logs 200 to the console
```

In this example, the y variable is only accessible within the nested block while z variable is accessible outside the block.

Function Expressions

In addition to function declarations, JavaScript also allows us to create functions using function expressions. Function expressions assign a function to a variable.

For example, the following code creates a function expression called addDollarSign and assigns it to the variable addDollarSign:

```
const addDollarSign = function(value) {
  return '$' + value;
};

console.log(addDollarSign(100)); // Logs '$100' to the console
```

Function expressions can be invoked in the same way as function declarations.

Hoisting

Hoisting is the process of moving all function and variable declarations to the top of the current scope before the code is executed. This means that function declarations are available before the code is executed, but function expressions are not.

For example, the following code will work even though the addDollarSign function is called before it is declared:

```
console.log(addDollarSign(100)); // Logs '$100' to the console
```

```javascript
function addDollarSign(value) {
  return '$' + value;
}
```

However, the following code will not work because the `addPlusSign` function is not declared before it is called:

```javascript
console.log(addPlusSign(200)); // Error: addPlusSign is not defined

const addPlusSign = function(value) {
  return '+' + value;
};
```

Function Declarations vs Function Expressions

The main difference between function declarations and function expressions is that function declarations are hoisted, while function expressions are not. This means that function declarations can be called before they are declared, but function expressions cannot.

Another difference is that function declarations are added to the window object, while function expressions are not. This means that function declarations can be accessed from anywhere in the global scope, but function expressions cannot.

Arrow Functions

Arrow functions were introduced in JavaScript in 2015 as part of the ES2015 (ES6) update. They offer several advantages over traditional function declarations and expressions, including:

- **Compactness:** Arrow functions are more compact than traditional functions, making them easier to read and write.
- **Implicit return:** Arrow functions have an implicit return, meaning that you can omit the `return` keyword when returning a single expression.
- **Lexical scope:** Arrow functions use lexical scope, which means that they inherit the scope of the surrounding environment.

Functions and Scope

The syntax for an arrow function is as follows:

```
(parameters) => expression
```

For example, the following arrow function returns the sum of two numbers:

```
const add = (a, b) => a + b;
```

Implicit Return

If an arrow function only contains a single expression, you can omit the curly braces and the `return` keyword. For example, the following arrow function is equivalent to the previous example:

```
const add = (a, b) => a + b;
```

Lexical Scope

Arrow functions use lexical scope, which means that they inherit the scope of the surrounding environment. This is in contrast to traditional functions, which use dynamic scope.

For example, the following code demonstrates how arrow functions use lexical scope:

```
const outer = () => {
  const a = 10;

  const inner = () => {
    console.log(a); // Logs 10
  };

  inner();
};

outer();
```

In this example, the `inner` function has access to the variable `a` declared in the `outer` function, even though `a` is not declared within the `inner` function. This is because arrow functions use lexical scope, which means that they inherit the scope of the surrounding environment.

Single Parameter

If an arrow function only has a single parameter, you can omit the parentheses around the parameter. For example, the following arrow function is equivalent to the previous example:

```
const double = a => a * 2;
```

Returning Objects

When returning an object from an arrow function, you must surround the curly braces with parentheses. This is because the arrow points to the curly braces, which can be confusing when returning an object.

For example, the following arrow function returns an object with a `name` property:

```
const createObject = () => ({ name: "Brad" });
```

Arrow Functions in Callbacks

Arrow functions are commonly used in callbacks, which are functions passed as arguments to other functions.

For example, the following code uses an arrow function as a callback in the `forEach` method of an array:

```
const numbers = [1, 2, 3, 4, 5];

numbers.forEach((n) => console.log(n));
```

This code logs each number in the array to the console.

Advantages of Arrow Functions in Callbacks

Arrow functions offer several advantages when used in callbacks:

- **Compactness:** Arrow functions are more compact than traditional functions, making them easier to read and write.
- **Lexical scope:** Arrow functions use lexical scope, which means that they inherit the scope of the surrounding environment. This can be useful when accessing variables from the outer scope.
- **Implicit return:** Arrow functions have an implicit return, meaning that you can omit the `return` keyword when returning a single expression. This can make your code more concise and readable.

Immediately Invoked Function Expressions (IIFEs)

An immediately invoked function expression (IIFE) is a function that is declared and invoked at the same time. This is useful for avoiding global scope pollution, which occurs when variables are declared in the global scope and can be accessed by any part of the program.

Syntax

The syntax for an IIFE is as follows:

```js
(function() {
  // Function body
})();
```

The function is declared within the parentheses, and the parentheses are followed by a second set of parentheses to invoke the function.

The following code creates an IIFE that declares a variable called `user` and logs it to the console:

```js
(function() {
  const user = "Brad";
  console.log(user);
})();
```

This code will log "Brad" to the console without polluting the global scope.

You can also pass parameters to an IIFE. For example, the following code creates an IIFE that takes a name as a parameter and logs a greeting:

```javascript
(function(name) {
  console.log(`Hello, ${name}!`);
})("Sean");
```

This code will log "Hello, Sean!" to the console.

You can also give an IIFE a name. This can be useful for debugging purposes. For example, the following code creates a named IIFE called hello:

```javascript
function hello(name) {
  console.log(`Hello, ${name}!`);
}

hello("Sean");
```

This code will log "Hello, Sean!" to the console.

Advantages of IIFEs

IIFEs offer several advantages:

- **Avoid global scope pollution:** IIFEs prevent variables from being declared in the global scope, which can help to improve code organization and reduce the risk of conflicts.
- **Encapsulation:** IIFEs can be used to encapsulate code and data, making it easier to manage and reuse.
- **Modularity:** IIFEs can be used to create modular code that can be easily imported and reused in other parts of the program.

Recursion

Recursion is a technique in which a function calls itself. This can be useful for solving certain types of problems, such as finding the factorial of a number or traversing a tree data structure.

The following code creates a recursive function called `hello` that logs "Hello" to the console:

```
function hello() {
  console.log("Hello");
  hello();
}

hello();
```

This code will log "Hello" to the console indefinitely, until the browser crashes. This is because the function calls itself without any terminating condition.

Infinite Loops

An infinite loop is a loop that never ends. This can happen if a function calls itself without a terminating condition, or if a loop condition is always true.

The following code creates an infinite loop:

```
while (true) {
  console.log("Hello");
}
```

This code will log "Hello" to the console indefinitely, until the browser crashes.

To avoid infinite loops, it is important to ensure that all loops have a terminating condition. This means that the loop should stop executing when a certain condition is met.

Challenge 1: Convert Fahrenheit to Celsius

Create a function called `getCelsius` that takes a temperature in Fahrenheit as an argument and returns the temperature in Celsius. For bonus points, write it as a one-line arrow function.

Solution

```
const getCelsius = (fahrenheit) => (fahrenheit - 32) * 5 / 9;
```

This function takes a Fahrenheit temperature as an argument and returns the temperature in Celsius. The formula for converting Fahrenheit to Celsius is `(fahrenheit - 32) * 5 / 9`.

Challenge 2

Create an arrow function called `minMax` that takes in an array of numbers and returns an object with the minimum and the maximum numbers in the array.

Solution

```
const minMax = (arr) => {
  const min = Math.min(...arr);
  const max = Math.max(...arr);
  return { min, max };
};
```

This function uses the spread operator to spread the values of the array into separate arguments to the `Math.min` and `Math.max` methods. The result is an object with the minimum and maximum numbers in the array.

Example

```
const arr = [1, 2, 3, 4, 5];
const result = minMax(arr);
console.log(result); // { min: 1, max: 5 }
```

Challenge 3: Calculate the Area of a Rectangle

Create an IIFE (Immediately Invoked Function Expression) that takes in the length and width of a rectangle and outputs it to the console in a message as soon as the page loads.

Solution

```
(() => {
  const length = 10;
```

```
  const width = 5;
  const area = length * width;
  const output = `The area of a rectangle with a length of $
{length} and a width of ${width} is ${area}.`;
  console.log(output);
})();
```

This IIFE creates a function that is immediately invoked when the page loads. The function takes in the length and width of a rectangle and calculates the area. It then logs a message to the console with the calculated area.

When the page loads, the following message will be logged to the console:

```
The area of a rectangle with a length of 10 and a width of 5
is 50.
```

Execution Context

The execution context is the environment in which JavaScript code is executed. It includes the following:

- The global object (e.g., `window` in a browser)
- The current function scope
- The variable environment (e.g., the variables that are available to the code)

The execution context is a special environment that is created by the JavaScript engine when code is executed. It includes the currently running code and everything that aids in its execution.

Global Execution Context

When a script is first loaded, the global execution context is created. This context includes the global object (e.g., `window` in a browser) and all of the variables and functions that are declared in the global scope.

Function Execution Context

When a function is invoked, a new execution context is created for that function. This context includes the function's scope and the global object. The function's scope includes the variables and functions that are declared within the function.

Memory Creation Phase

When an execution context is created, the memory creation phase occurs. During this phase, the following actions take place:

- The global object is created.
- The `this` object is created and bound to the global object.
- The memory heap is set up for storing variables and function references.

- All variables and function references are set to undefined.

Execution Phase

After the memory creation phase, the execution phase begins. During this phase, the code is executed line by line. As each line of code is executed, the following actions may occur:

- Variables are declared and assigned values.
- Functions are declared and stored in the memory heap.
- Function calls are made.
- Code blocks are executed.

Consider the following code:

```
var x = 10;

function add(a, b) {
   return a + b;
}

console.log(add(x, 5));
```

When this code is executed, the following execution contexts are created:

- **Global Execution Context:** This context includes the global object and the variable x.
- **Function Execution Context for add:** This context includes the function's scope and the global object. The function's scope includes the parameters a and b.

During the memory creation phase, the variable x is set to undefined in the global execution context. During the execution phase, the value of x is assigned to 10.

When the add function is invoked, a new execution context is created for the function. During the memory creation phase, the parameters a and b are set to `undefined`. During the execution phase, the values of a and b are assigned to 10 and 5, respectively.

The add function returns the value 15, which is then logged to the console.

Execution Context: Step-by-Step Walkthrough

Let's walk through the execution of the following code line by line to illustrate the concept of execution contexts:

```javascript
var x = 100;
var y = 50;

function getSum(n1, n2) {
  var sum = n1 + n2;
  return sum;
}

var sum1 = getSum(x, y);
```

Global Execution Context

- **Memory Creation Phase:**
    - Variable x is allocated in memory and set to `undefined`.
    - Variable y is allocated in memory and set to `undefined`.
    - Function getSum is allocated in memory.
    - Variable sum1 is allocated in memory and set to `undefined`.
- **Execution Phase:**
    - Variable x is assigned the value 100.
    - Variable y is assigned the value 50.
    - Function getSum is invoked, creating a new execution context.

Function Execution Context for getSum

- **Memory Creation Phase:**

- Variables n1 and n2 are allocated in memory and set to undefined.
- Variable sum is allocated in memory and set to undefined.
- **Execution Phase:**
  - Variables n1 and n2 are assigned the values of x and y, respectively (100 and 50).
  - Variable sum is assigned the value 150 (100 + 50).
  - Function getSum returns the value 150.
  - Variable sum1 is assigned the return value of getSum (150).

Execution Context: Call Stack

In addition to the execution context, we also have the call stack. The call stack is a data structure that keeps track of the currently executing functions.

Last In, First Out (LIFO)

The call stack operates on a LIFO (Last In, First Out) principle. This means that the last function that was invoked is **the first one to be executed.**

When a function is invoked, it is pushed onto the call stack. When the function finishes executing, it is popped off the call stack.

Consider the following code:

```
function first() {
  console.log("First function");
}

function second() {
  console.log("Second function");
}

function third() {
  console.log("Third function");
}
```

```
first();
second();
third();
```

When this code is executed, the following sequence of events occurs:

1. `first()` is invoked and pushed onto the call stack.
2. `first()` executes and logs "First function".
3. `first()` finishes executing and is popped off the call stack.
4. `second()` is invoked and pushed onto the call stack.
5. `second()` executes and logs "Second function".
6. `second()` finishes executing and is popped off the call stack.
7. `third()` is invoked and pushed onto the call stack.
8. `third()` executes and logs "Third function".
9. `third()` finishes executing and is popped off the call stack.

Importance of the Call Stack

The call stack is important because it allows us to track the flow of execution in our code. It also helps us to debug errors, as we can see which functions were called and in what order.

Let's demonstrate the call stack in the browser using the two code examples we discussed earlier.

Example 1: Running Functions in Sequence

```
first();
second();
third();
```

1. Set a breakpoint at the first function call.
2. Reload the page.
3. Click the "Step" button to execute the first function.
4. Observe the call stack in the browser's Sources tab. You will see `first` on top of the global execution context.
5. Continue stepping through the code.

6. You will see `second` and then `third` being pushed onto and popped off the call stack.

Example 2: Nested Function Calls

```
first();
second();
  third();
```

1. Set a breakpoint at the first function call.
2. Reload the page.
3. Click the "Step" button to execute the first function.
4. Observe the call stack. You will see `first` on top of the global execution context.
5. Step into the second function.
6. You will see `second` on top of `first`.
7. Step into the third function.
8. You will see `third` on top of `second`.
9. Continue stepping through the code.
10. You will see `third`, `second`, and then `first` being popped off the call stack.

These examples illustrate how the call stack tracks the flow of execution in our code. It allows us to see which functions are currently running and in what order.

Control Flow with If Statements

If statements allow us to control the flow of our code based on whether a condition is true or false. The syntax is:

```
if (condition) {
  // Code to execute if condition is true
}
```

Comparison Operators

We can use comparison operators to evaluate expressions and determine if they are true or false. Some common operators include:

- `==` and `===`: Equality (loose and strict)
- `!=` and `!==`: Inequality (loose and strict)
- `<`: Less than
- `<=`: Less than or equal to
- `>`: Greater than
- `>=`: Greater than or equal to

Example:

```
const x = 10;
const y = 5;

if (x > y) {
  console.log("x is greater than y");
} else {
  console.log("x is not greater than y");
}
```

Output:

```
x is greater than y
```

Scope in If Statements

If statements create their own scope, meaning variables declared within the block are only accessible within that block.

Example:

```
if (x > y) {
  let z = 20;
  console.log(z); // 20
}

console.log(z); // ReferenceError: z is not defined
```

Shorthand If Statements

We can use shorthand if statements to write concise code. The syntax is:

```
if (condition) statement;
else statement;
```

Example:

```
const x = 10;
const y = 5;

if (x > y) console.log("x is greater than y");
else console.log("x is not greater than y");
```

Output:

```
x is greater than y
```

Else If Statements

Else if statements allow us to test multiple conditions and execute different code blocks based on the result. The syntax is:

```
if (condition1) {
  // Code to execute if condition1 is true
} else if (condition2) {
```

```
  // Code to execute if condition2 is true
} else {
  // Code to execute if all conditions are false
}
```

Example:

```
const hour = new Date().getHours();

if (hour < 12) {
  console.log("Good morning");
} else if (hour < 18) {
  console.log("Good afternoon");
} else {
  console.log("Good evening");
}
```

Output:

```
Good morning
```

Nested If Statements

We can nest if statements to create more complex conditions. The syntax is:

```
if (condition1) {
  // Code to execute if condition1 is true
  if (condition2) {
    // Code to execute if condition2 is true
  }
}
```

Example:

```
const hour = new Date().getHours();

if (hour < 12) {
  console.log("Good morning");
  if (hour === 6) {
    console.log("Wake up");
```

```
  }
} else if (hour >= 20) {
  console.log("Good night");
  console.log("ZZZZZZZZZZZZ");
}
```

Output:

```
Good morning
Wake up
```

Multiple Conditions in a Single If Statement

We can use the logical AND (&&) operator to combine multiple conditions in a single if statement. The syntax is:

```
if (condition1 && condition2) {
  // Code to execute if both conditions are true
}
```

Example:

```
const hour = new Date().getHours();

if (hour >= 7 && hour < 15) {
  console.log("Good morning");
}
```

Output:

```
Good morning
```

The logical OR operator (||) is used to combine multiple conditions in a single if statement. The syntax is:

```
if (condition1 || condition2) {
  // Code to execute if either condition1 or condition2 is true
}
```

Example:

Control Flow with If Statements

```javascript
const hour = new Date().getHours();

if (hour === 6 || hour === 20) {
  console.log("Brush your teeth");
}
```

Output:

```
Brush your teeth
```

Switches

Switches are another way to evaluate expressions and values. The syntax is:

```
switch (expression) {
  case value1:
    // Code to execute if expression equals value1
    break;
  case value2:
    // Code to execute if expression equals value2
    break;
  default:
    // Code to execute if expression does not match any case
}
```

Example:

```
const month = new Date().getMonth();

switch (month) {
  case 0:
    console.log("It is January");
    break;
  case 1:
    console.log("It is February");
    break;
  case 2:
    console.log("It is March");
    break;
  default:
    console.log("It is not January, February, or March");
}
```

Output:

```
It is January
```

Switches with Ranges

Switches can also be used to evaluate ranges of values. The syntax is:

```
switch (expression) {
  case value1:
  case value2:
  case value3:
    // Code to execute if expression equals value1, value2, or value3
    break;
  default:
    // Code to execute if expression does not match any case
}
```

Example:

```
const hour = new Date().getHours();

switch (hour) {
  case 7:
  case 8:
  case 9:
  case 10:
  case 11:
    console.log("It is morning");
    break;
  case 12:
  case 13:
  case 14:
  case 15:
  case 16:
    console.log("It is afternoon");
    break;
  default:
    console.log("It is not morning or afternoon");
}
```

Output:

```
It is morning
```

Calculator Challenge

Create a function called `calculator` that takes in three parameters: num1, num2, and operator. The operator can be one of the following: +, -, *, or /. The function should return the result of the calculation. If any other operator is passed in, the function should return an error message.

Hint: You can use an if statement or a switch statement to handle the different operators.

Example:

```
calculator(5, 2, "+"); // 7
calculator(5, 2, "-"); // 3
calculator(5, 2, "*"); // 10
calculator(5, 2, "/"); // 2.5
calculator(5, 2, "**"); // Error: Invalid operator
```

Solution using a switch statement:
```
function calculator(num1, num2, operator) {
  let result;

  switch (operator) {
    case "+":
      result = num1 + num2;
      break;
    case "-":
      result = num1 - num2;
      break;
    case "*":
      result = num1 * num2;
      break;
    case "/":
      result = num1 / num2;
      break;
    default:
      result = "Invalid operator";
```

```
    }

    console.log(result);
    return result;
}
```

Truthy and Falsy Values

In JavaScript, there are two special values called `true` and `false`. These values are used to represent boolean conditions. However, there are other values that are considered "truthy" or "falsy" when used in boolean contexts.

Falsy Values:

- `false`
- `0`
- `""` (empty string)
- `null`
- `undefined`
- `NaN` (Not a Number)

Truthy Values:

- `true`
- Any non-zero number
- Any non-empty string
- Any object (including arrays and functions)

Example:

```javascript
const x = false;

if (x) {
  console.log("This is truthy");
} else {
  console.log("This is falsy");
}
```

Output:

```
This is falsy
```

Note:

- Anything that is not falsy is considered truthy.
- When a value is passed into an if statement, it is coerced into a boolean value.
- Some values that may seem falsy, such as 0 and "", are actually considered truthy in JavaScript.

Confusing Truthy Values:

- 0 is truthy, even though it is a number that is equal to zero.
- An empty string ("") is truthy, even though it contains no characters.
- An object is truthy, even if it is an empty object ({}).

Empty Arrays and Objects:

- Empty arrays and objects are considered truthy in JavaScript. This can be confusing because you might expect them to be falsy since they contain no elements or properties.
- To check if an array or object is empty, you can use the `length` property or the `Object.keys()` method, respectively.

Example:

```
const posts = [];

if (posts) {
  console.log("List posts");
} else {
  console.log("No posts");
}
```

Output:

```
List posts
```

Zero and Empty Strings:

- Zero (0) and empty strings ("") are truthy values. This can also be confusing, especially when validating form input.
- To check if a value is truly empty, you can use the === operator to compare it to "" or 0.

Example:

```
const children = 0;

if (children !== 0) {
  console.log("You have " + children + " children");
} else {
  console.log("Please enter the number of children");
}
```

Output:

```
Please enter the number of children
```

NaN:

- NaN (Not a Number) is a special value that represents an invalid number. It is considered falsy in JavaScript.
- You can use the isNaN() function to check if a value is NaN.

Example:

```
const num = NaN;

if (!isNaN(num)) {
  console.log("This is a valid number");
} else {
  console.log("This is not a valid number");
}
```

Output:

```
This is not a valid number
```

Empty Arrays:

- Empty arrays are truthy in JavaScript. To check if an array is empty, use the `length` property.

Example:

```javascript
const posts = [];

if (posts.length === 0) {
  console.log("No posts to list");
} else {
  console.log("List posts");
}
```

Output:

```
No posts to list
```

Empty Objects:

- Empty objects are also truthy. To check if an object is empty, use the `Object.keys()` method to get an array of its keys. If the array is empty, the object is empty.

Example:

```javascript
const user = {};

if (Object.keys(user).length === 0) {
  console.log("No user");
} else {
  console.log("List user");
}
```

Output:

```
No user
```

Loose Equality (==) vs. Strict Equality (===)

- Loose equality (==) compares values without considering their types. This can lead to unexpected results, especially when comparing falsy values.
- Strict equality (===) compares both the values and types of operands. It is recommended to always use strict equality to avoid confusion.

Example:

```
console.log(false == 0); // true (loose equality)
console.log(false === 0); // false (strict equality)
```

Note: It is generally recommended to use strict equality (===) in JavaScript to avoid potential confusion and errors.

AND (&&)

- The AND operator (&&) evaluates multiple expressions and returns `true` only if all expressions are `true`.
- If any expression is `false`, the entire expression evaluates to `false`.

Example:

```
console.log(10 > 20 && 30 > 15); // false
console.log(10 < 20 && 30 > 15); // true
```

OR (||)

- The OR operator (||) evaluates multiple expressions and returns true if any expression is `true`.
- If all expressions are `false`, the entire expression evaluates to `false`.

Example:

```
console.log(10 > 20 || 30 > 15); // true
console.log(10 < 20 || 30 < 15); // false
```

Getting the First Non-Falsy Value

The AND operator can be used to get the first non-falsy value in a series of expressions.

Example:

```
const posts = ["post one", "post two"];

const firstPost = posts[0] || posts[1];

console.log(firstPost); // "post one"
```

In this example, posts[0] is not falsy, so it is returned. If posts[0] were falsy, posts[1] would be returned instead.

Conditional Rendering with AND (&&)

The AND operator can be used for conditional rendering in React and other front-end frameworks.

Example:

```
const posts = ["post one", "post two"];

const renderFirstPost = () => {
  if (posts.length > 0) {
    return <div>{posts[0]}</div>;
  }
};
```

In this example, the renderFirstPost function returns a div containing the first post only if the posts array is not empty.

OR (||) and Nullish Coalescing Operator (??)

- The OR operator (||) returns the first truthy value or the last value.
- The nullish coalescing operator (??) returns the right-hand operand if the left-hand operand is null or undefined.

Example: Default Value with Nullish Coalescing Operator

```
const user = {
  name: "John Doe",
  age: null,
};

const age = user.age ?? 25;

console.log(age); // 25
```

In this example, the `age` variable is assigned the value of `user.age` if it is not `null` or `undefined`. Otherwise, it is assigned the default value of 25.

Logical Assignment Operators

Logical assignment operators are shorthand for common conditional assignments.

OR Assignment (||=)

- Assigns the right-hand operand to the left-hand operand only if the left-hand operand is falsy.

Example:
```
let a = false;
a ||= 10; // a is now 10
```

AND Assignment (&&=)

- Assigns the right-hand operand to the left-hand operand only if the left-hand operand is truthy.

Example:
```
let b = 20;
b &&= 10; // b remains 20
```

Nullish Coalescing Assignment (??=)

- Assigns the right-hand operand to the left-hand operand only if the left-hand operand is `null` or `undefined`.

Example:

```javascript
let c = null;
c ??= 10; // c is now 10
```

Example: Default Value with OR Assignment

```javascript
const user = {
  name: "John Doe",
  age: null,
};

user.age ||= 25;

console.log(user.age); // 25
```

In this example, the `age` property of the `user` object is assigned the value of 25 if it is `null` or `undefined`.

Example: Default Value with Nullish Coalescing Assignment

```javascript
const user = {
  name: "John Doe",
  age: null,
};

user.age ??= 25;

console.log(user.age); // 25
```

In this example, the `age` property of the `user` object is assigned the value of 25 if it is `null` or `undefined`. This is useful for setting default values without having to check for `null` and `undefined` explicitly.

Ternary Operator

The ternary operator is a concise way to write conditional statements. It has three parts:

1. **Condition:** The expression that is evaluated to determine which branch of the operator to execute.
2. **True Branch:** The expression that is executed if the condition is true.
3. **False Branch:** The expression that is executed if the condition is false.

Syntax:

```
condition ? trueBranch : falseBranch
```

Example:

```
const age = 19;
const canVote = age >= 18 ? "You can vote" : "You cannot vote";

console.log(canVote); // "You can vote"
```

Example: Assigning Conditional Value to Variable

```
let message;

const isLoggedIn = true;
message = isLoggedIn ? "Welcome back!" : "Please log in";

console.log(message); // "Welcome back!"
```

In this example, the `message` variable is assigned the value "Welcome back!" if `isLoggedIn` is `true`, and "Please log in" otherwise.

Ternary Operator with Multiple Statements

The ternary operator can be used to execute multiple statements in both the true and false branches. To do this, enclose the statements in parentheses.

Example:

```javascript
const auth = true;
const redirect = auth
  ? (alert("Welcome to the dashboard"), "/dashboard")
  : (alert("Access denied"), "/login");

console.log(redirect); // "/dashboard"
```

In this example, if auth is true, the ternary operator executes the alert("Welcome to the dashboard") statement and sets redirect to "/dashboard". If auth is false, the ternary operator executes the alert("Access denied") statement and sets redirect to "/login".

Example: Conditional Redirection

```javascript
const isLoggedIn = true;
const redirectUrl = isLoggedIn ? "/dashboard" : "/login";

window.location.href = redirectUrl;
```

In this example, the redirectUrl variable is set to "/dashboard" if the user is logged in (i.e., isLoggedIn is true), and to "/login" otherwise. The window.location.href property is then set to redirectUrl, causing the browser to redirect the user to the appropriate page.

Ternary Operator with Shorthand

The ternary operator can be used with a shorthand syntax when there is no else branch. The && (and) operator can be used to conditionally execute a statement if the condition is true.

Example:

```javascript
const auth = true;
const message = auth && console.log("Welcome to the dashboard");

console.log(message); // "Welcome to the dashboard"
```

In this example, the `message` variable is set to the result of the `auth && console.log("Welcome to the dashboard")` expression. Since `auth` is `true`, the `console.log("Welcome to the dashboard")` statement is executed and the message "Welcome to the dashboard" is printed to the console. If `auth` were `false`, the `console.log("Welcome to the dashboard")` statement would not be executed and `message` would be set to `undefined`.

Example: Conditional Logging

```javascript
const isDebugMode = true;

isDebugMode && console.log("Debug message");
```

In this example, the `console.log("Debug message")` statement is only executed if `isDebugMode` is `true`. This is useful for logging debug messages that should only be displayed when debugging the application.

For Loop

A for loop is a control structure that allows you to iterate over a sequence of values. It has the following syntax:

```
for (initialExpression; conditionExpression; incrementExpression) {
  // Code to be executed
}
```

- **Initial expression:** Initializes a variable or counter to use within the loop.
- **Condition expression:** The condition that the loop will continue to run as long as it is met.
- **Increment expression:** Executed after each iteration of the loop, typically to increment the counter.

Example:

```
for (let i = 0; i <= 10; i++) {
  console.log("Number " + i);
}
```

In this example, the loop will iterate from `i = 0` to `i = 10`. The `console.log("Number " + i)` statement will be executed on each iteration, printing the message "Number 0" to "Number 10" to the console.

Example: Iterating Over an Array

```
const numbers = [1, 2, 3, 4, 5];

for (let i = 0; i < numbers.length; i++) {
  console.log(numbers[i]);
}
```

In this example, the loop will iterate over the `numbers` array, printing each element to the console.

Nested Loops

Nested loops are loops within loops. They can be used to iterate over multi-dimensional data structures or to perform complex calculations.

Example:

```
for (let i = 1; i <= 10; i++) {
  console.log("Number " + i);
  for (let j = 1; j <= 10; j++) {
    console.log("   " + i + " times " + j + " equals " + (i * j));
  }
}
```

In this example, the outer loop iterates from `i = 1` to `i = 10`. For each value of `i`, the inner loop iterates from `j = 1` to `j = 10`. The `console.log` statement within the inner loop prints the multiplication table for `i`.

Example: Iterating Over a 2D Array

```
const matrix = [
  [1, 2, 3],
  [4, 5, 6],
  [7, 8, 9],
];

for (let i = 0; i < matrix.length; i++) {
  for (let j = 0; j < matrix[i].length; j++) {
    console.log(matrix[i][j]);
  }
}
```

In this example, the outer loop iterates over the rows of the `matrix` array. For each row, the inner loop iterates over the columns of the row. The `console.log` statement within the inner loop prints each element of the matrix.

Example: Modifying Array Elements

```js
const names = ["John", "Tim", "Sarah"];

for (let i = 0; i < names.length; i++) {
  if (i === 2) {
    names[i] += " is the best";
  } else {
    console.log(names[i]);
  }
}
```

In this example, the `for` loop iterates over the `names` array. If the current index `i` is equal to 2, the element at that index is modified to include the string `" is the best"`. Otherwise, the element is simply printed to the console.

Infinite Loops

An infinite loop is a loop that continues to execute indefinitely. This can happen if the loop condition is always true or if the loop body does not properly increment the loop variable.

Example:

```js
for (let i = 0; i < Infinity; i++) {
  console.log("This loop will never end!");
}
```

In this example, the loop condition `i < Infinity` is always true, so the loop will continue to execute until the browser crashes.

Break and Continue Statements

The `break` and `continue` statements allow you to control the flow of a loop.

The `break` statement immediately exits the loop, regardless of the loop condition. It's often used when a specific condition is met and you want to stop the loop early.

Example:

```
for (let i = 0; i <= 20; i++) {
  console.log(i);
  if (i === 15) {
    break;
  }
}
```

In this example, the loop will print numbers from 0 to 15, and then exit the loop when `i` reaches 15.

The `continue` statement skips the remaining code in the current iteration of the loop and continues to the next iteration. It's often used when you want to skip a specific condition within the loop.

Example:

```
for (let i = 0; i <= 20; i++) {
  if (i === 13) {
    console.log("Skipping 13");
    continue;
  }
  console.log(i);
}
```

In this example, the loop will print numbers from 0 to 12, skip 13, and then continue printing numbers from 14 to 20.

While and Do-While Loops

The `while` and `do-while` loops are similar to the `for` loop, but they have different syntax.

The `while` loop executes a block of code as long as a specified condition is true.

Example:
```
let i = 0;
while (i <= 20) {
  console.log(i);
  i++;
}
```

The `do-while` loop executes a block of code at least once, and then continues to execute the block as long as a specified condition is true.

Example:
```
let i = 0;
do {
  console.log(i);
  i++;
} while (i <= 20);
```

Using While Loops with Arrays

While loops can also be used to iterate over arrays, similar to for loops.

Example:
```
const array = [10, 20, 30, 40];
let i = 0;
while (i < array.length) {
  console.log(array[i]);
  i++;
}
```

Nested While Loops

While loops can be nested, just like for loops.

Example:
```
let i = 1;
while (i <= 5) {
  console.log("Number: " + i);
  let j = 1;
  while (j <= 5) {
    console.log(i + " times " + j + " is " + (i * j));
    j++;
  }
  i++;
}
```

When to Use Do-While Loops

Do-while loops are useful when you want to ensure that the loop body is executed at least once, regardless of the condition. For example, you might use a do-while loop to prompt the user for input until they enter a valid value.

Key Points:

- Do-while loops always execute the loop body at least once, even if the condition is false.
- This is in contrast to while loops, which only execute the loop body if the condition is true.
- Do-while loops are useful when you want to ensure that the loop body is executed at least once, regardless of the condition.

FizzBuzz Challenge

Instructions:

- Print or log the numbers from 1 to 100.
- For multiples of three, print "Fizz" instead of the number.
- For multiples of five, print "Buzz" instead of the number.
- For numbers that are multiples of both three and five, print "FizzBuzz".

Hints:

- You can use a loop to print the numbers.
- You can use conditional statements to check for multiples of three and five.
- You can use the modulus operator (%) to get the remainder of a number.

Solution (Using a For Loop):

```
for (let i = 1; i <= 100; i++) {
  if (i % 3 === 0 && i % 5 === 0) {
    console.log("FizzBuzz");
  } else if (i % 3 === 0) {
    console.log("Fizz");
  } else if (i % 5 === 0) {
    console.log("Buzz");
  } else {
    console.log(i);
  }
}
```

Solution (Using a While Loop):

```
let i = 1;
while (i <= 100) {
  if (i % 3 === 0 && i % 5 === 0) {
    console.log("FizzBuzz");
```

```
  } else if (i % 3 === 0) {
    console.log("Fizz");
  } else if (i % 5 === 0) {
    console.log("Buzz");
  } else {
    console.log(i);
  }
  i++;
}
```

Solution (Using a For Loop):

```
for (let i = 1; i <= 100; i++) {
  if (i % 3 === 0 && i % 5 === 0) {
    console.log("FizzBuzz");
  } else if (i % 3 === 0) {
    console.log("Fizz");
  } else if (i % 5 === 0) {
    console.log("Buzz");
  } else {
    console.log(i);
  }
}
```

Shorter Solution Using Modulus 15:

```
for (let i = 1; i <= 100; i++) {
  if (i % 15 === 0) {
    console.log("FizzBuzz");
  } else if (i % 3 === 0) {
    console.log("Fizz");
  } else if (i % 5 === 0) {
    console.log("Buzz");
  } else {
    console.log(i);
  }
}
```

Since 3 times 5 is 15, any number that is divisible by 15 is also divisible by both 3 and 5. Therefore, we can check for divisibility by 15 first, and if that condition is not met, we can check for divisibility by 3 and 5 separately.

For-Of Loop

The for-of loop is a newer way to iterate over iterable objects, such as arrays, strings, maps, and sets. It is a cleaner and more modern alternative to the traditional for loop or while loop.

Syntax:

```
for (const variable of iterable) {
  // Loop body
}
```

Example (Iterating over an Array):

```
const items = ["Book", "Table", "Chair", "Kite"];

for (const item of items) {
  console.log(item);
}
```

Output:

```
Book
Table
Chair
Kite
```

Example (Iterating over an Array of Objects):

```
const users = [
  { name: "Brad" },
  { name: "Kate" },
  { name: "Steve" },
];

for (const user of users) {
  console.log(user.name);
}
```

Output:

```
Brad
Kate
Steve
```

Example (Iterating over a String):

```javascript
const str = "Hello World";

for (const char of str) {
  console.log(char);
}
```

Output:
```
H
e
l
l
o
 
W
o
r
l
d
```

Key Points:

- The for-of loop is a convenient and concise way to iterate over iterable objects.
- It eliminates the need to manually initialize and increment a loop variable.
- It provides direct access to each element or character in the iterable object.
- It is generally preferred over traditional for loops or while loops for iterating over arrays, strings, and other iterable objects.

High-Order Array Methods

forEach()

High-order array methods are methods that take an array as an argument and return a new array or perform an operation on the original array. One of the most common high-order array methods is forEach().

Syntax:

`array.forEach(callbackFunction);`

Callback Function:

The callback function is a function that is passed to the forEach() method. It is called for each element in the array. The callback function takes the following arguments:

- **element:** The current element in the array.
- **index:** The index of the current element in the array.
- **array:** The original array.

Example:

```
const socials = ["Twitter", "LinkedIn", "Facebook", "Instagram"];

socials.forEach((social) => {
  console.log(social);
});
```

Output:

```
Twitter
LinkedIn
Facebook
Instagram
```

Key Points:

- The forEach() method iterates over each element in an array and calls a callback function for each element.
- The callback function can access the current element, its index, and the original array.
- The forEach() method does not return anything. It simply performs an operation on each element in the array.
- The forEach() method is commonly used to iterate over arrays and perform operations on each element, such as logging them to the console or modifying them.

forEach() with Additional Parameters

In addition to the element parameter, the forEach() callback function can also receive two additional parameters:

- **index:** The index of the current element in the array.
- **array:** The original array.

Example:

```javascript
const socials = ["Twitter", "LinkedIn", "Facebook", "Instagram"];

socials.forEach((social, index, array) => {
  console.log(`Item: ${social}, Index: ${index}, Array: ${array}`);
});
```

Output:

```
Item: Twitter, Index: 0, Array: [ 'Twitter', 'LinkedIn', 'Facebook', 'Instagram' ]
Item: LinkedIn, Index: 1, Array: [ 'Twitter', 'LinkedIn', 'Facebook', 'Instagram' ]
Item: Facebook, Index: 2, Array: [ 'Twitter', 'LinkedIn', 'Facebook', 'Instagram' ]
```

```
Item: Instagram, Index: 3, Array: [ 'Twitter', 'LinkedIn',
'Facebook', 'Instagram' ]
```

Named Callback Functions

Instead of using an anonymous callback function, you can also pass in a named function to the forEach() method.

Example:

```
function logSocial(social) {
  console.log(social);
}

const socials = ["Twitter", "LinkedIn", "Facebook",
"Instagram"];

socials.forEach(logSocial);
```

Output:

```
Twitter
LinkedIn
Facebook
Instagram
```

forEach() with Objects

The forEach() method can also be used to iterate over arrays of objects.

Example:

```
const socialObjects = [
  { name: "Twitter", url: "https://twitter.com" },
  { name: "LinkedIn", url: "https://linkedin.com" },
  { name: "Facebook", url: "https://facebook.com" },
  { name: "Instagram", url: "https://instagram.com" },
];

socialObjects.forEach((social) => {
```

```
    console.log(`Name: ${social.name}, URL: ${social.url}`);
});
```

Output:

```
Name: Twitter, URL: https://twitter.com
Name: LinkedIn, URL: https://linkedin.com
Name: Facebook, URL: https://facebook.com
Name: Instagram, URL: https://instagram.com
```

filter()

The filter() method is a high-order array method that returns a new array containing only the elements that pass a given test.

Syntax:

```
array.filter(callbackFunction);
```

Parameters:

- **callbackFunction:** A function that takes an element of the array as an argument and returns a boolean value.

Return Value:

An array containing the elements that passed the test.

Example:

```
const numbers = [1, 2, 3, 4, 5, 6, 7, 8, 9, 10];

const evenNumbers = numbers.filter((number) => {
   return number % 2 === 0;
});

console.log(evenNumbers); // [2, 4, 6, 8, 10]
```

In this example, the filter() method is used to create a new array called evenNumbers that contains only the even numbers from the numbers array. The callback function takes a single parameter, number, which represents each element of the numbers array. The callback function returns true if the number is even (i.e., number % 2 === 0), and false otherwise.

Note: The filter() method does not modify the original array.

filter() with Complex Objects

The filter() method can also be used to filter arrays of complex objects.

Example:

```
const companies = [
  { name: "Company 1", category: "Retail", startDate: "1980-01-01", endDate: "2000-12-31" },
  { name: "Company 2", category: "Retail", startDate: "1990-01-01", endDate: "2010-12-31" },
  { name: "Company 3", category: "Tech", startDate: "2000-01-01", endDate: "2020-12-31" },
  { name: "Company 4", category: "Retail", startDate: "2010-01-01", endDate: "2022-12-31" },
  { name: "Company 5", category: "Tech", startDate: "2015-01-01", endDate: "2025-12-31" },
  { name: "Company 6", category: "Retail", startDate: "2020-01-01", endDate: "2030-12-31" },
  { name: "Company 7", category: "Tech", startDate: "2022-01-01", endDate: "2032-12-31" },
  { name: "Company 8", category: "Retail", startDate: "1970-01-01", endDate: "1990-12-31" },
  { name: "Company 9", category: "Retail", startDate: "2005-01-01", endDate: "2015-12-31" },
];

// Get retail companies
const retailCompanies = companies.filter((company) => {
  return company.category === "Retail";
});

console.log(retailCompanies); // [
//   { name: "Company 2", category: "Retail", startDate:
```

```
//              "1990-01-01", endDate: "2010-12-31" },
//      { name: "Company 4", category: "Retail", startDate:
"2010-01-01", endDate: "2022-12-31" },
//      { name: "Company 6", category: "Retail", startDate:
"2020-01-01", endDate: "2030-12-31" },
//      { name: "Company 8", category: "Retail", startDate:
"1970-01-01", endDate: "1990-12-31" },
//      { name: "Company 9", category: "Retail", startDate:
"2005-01-01", endDate: "2015-12-31" },
// ]

// Get companies that started in or after 1980 and ended in
or before 2005
const earlyCompanies = companies.filter((company) => {
  return company.startDate >= "1980-01-01" && company.endDate
<= "2005-12-31";
});

console.log(earlyCompanies); // [
//      { name: "Company 1", category: "Retail", startDate:
"1980-01-01", endDate: "2000-12-31" },
//      { name: "Company 2", category: "Retail", startDate:
"1990-01-01", endDate: "2010-12-31" },
//      { name: "Company 8", category: "Retail", startDate:
"1970-01-01", endDate: "1990-12-31" },
// ]
```

In the first example, we filter the companies array to get only the retail companies. In the second example, we filter the companies array to get only the companies that started in or after 1980 and ended in or before 2005.

map() with Complex Objects

The map() method can also be used to transform arrays of complex objects.

Example:

```javascript
const companies = [
  { name: "Company 1", category: "Retail", startDate: "1980-01-01", endDate: "2000-12-31" },
  { name: "Company 2", category: "Retail", startDate: "1990-01-01", endDate: "2010-12-31" },
  { name: "Company 3", category: "Tech", startDate: "2000-01-01", endDate: "2020-12-31" },
  { name: "Company 4", category: "Retail", startDate: "2010-01-01", endDate: "2022-12-31" },
  { name: "Company 5", category: "Tech", startDate: "2015-01-01", endDate: "2025-12-31" },
  { name: "Company 6", category: "Retail", startDate: "2020-01-01", endDate: "2030-12-31" },
  { name: "Company 7", category: "Tech", startDate: "2022-01-01", endDate: "2032-12-31" },
  { name: "Company 8", category: "Retail", startDate: "1970-01-01", endDate: "1990-12-31" },
  { name: "Company 9", category: "Retail", startDate: "2005-01-01", endDate: "2015-12-31" },
];

// Get company names
const companyNames = companies.map((company) => {
  return company.name;
});

console.log(companyNames); // [
//   "Company 1",
//   "Company 2",
//   "Company 3",
//   "Company 4",
//   "Company 5",
//   "Company 6",
//   "Company 7",
//   "Company 8",
//   "Company 9",
// ]

// Get company categories
```

```javascript
const companyCategories = companies.map((company) => {
  return company.category;
});

console.log(companyCategories); // [
//     "Retail",
//     "Retail",
//     "Tech",
//     "Retail",
//     "Tech",
//     "Retail",
//     "Tech",
//     "Retail",
//     "Retail",
// ]

// Get company start dates
const companyStartDates = companies.map((company) => {
  return company.startDate;
});

console.log(companyStartDates); // [
//     "1980-01-01",
//     "1990-01-01",
//     "2000-01-01",
//     "2010-01-01",
//     "2015-01-01",
//     "2020-01-01",
//     "2022-01-01",
//     "1970-01-01",
//     "2005-01-01",
// ]
```

In the first example, we map the companies array to get an array of company names. In the second example, we map the companies array to get an array of company categories. In the third example, we map the companies array to get an array of company start dates. C

map() with Arrays of Objects

The map() method can also be used to transform arrays of objects.

Example:

```javascript
// Get company names
const companyNames = companies.map((company) => {
  return company.name;
});

console.log(companyNames); // [
//    "Company 1",
//    "Company 2",
//    "Company 3",
//    "Company 4",
//    "Company 5",
//    "Company 6",
//    "Company 7",
//    "Company 8",
//    "Company 9",
// ]

// Get company categories
const companyCategories = companies.map((company) => {
  return company.category;
});

console.log(companyCategories); // [
//    "Retail",
//    "Retail",
//    "Tech",
//    "Retail",
//    "Tech",
//    "Retail",
//    "Tech",
//    "Retail",
//    "Retail",
// ]
```

```javascript
// Get company info (name and category)
const companyInfo = companies.map((company) => {
  return {
    name: company.name,
    category: company.category,
  };
});

console.log(companyInfo); // [
//   { name: "Company 1", category: "Retail" },
//   { name: "Company 2", category: "Retail" },
//   { name: "Company 3", category: "Tech" },
//   { name: "Company 4", category: "Retail" },
//   { name: "Company 5", category: "Tech" },
//   { name: "Company 6", category: "Retail" },
//   { name: "Company 7", category: "Tech" },
//   { name: "Company 8", category: "Retail" },
//   { name: "Company 9", category: "Retail" },
// ]
```

In the first example, we map the companies array to get an array of company names. In the second example, we map the companies array to get an array of company categories. In the third example, we map the companies array to get an array of objects, each of which contains the company name and category.

Chaining map() Methods

The map() method can be chained to perform multiple transformations on an array.

Example:

```javascript
// Square and double each number
const squareAndDouble = numbers.map((number) => {
  return Math.sqrt(number) * 2;
});

console.log(squareAndDouble); // [
//   1.4142135623730951,
```

```
//    2.8284271247461903,
//    4.242640687119285,
//    5.656854249492381,
//    7.0710678118654755,
//    8.48528137423857,
//    9.899494936611665,
//    11.313708498984761,
//    12.727922061357856,
// ]
```

In this example, we chain two map() methods to first square each number and then double the result.

Long Version:

```
const squareAndDoubleTwo = numbers.map((number) => {
  const squareRoot = Math.sqrt(number);
  return squareRoot * 2;
});

console.log(squareAndDoubleTwo); // [
//    1.4142135623730951,
//    2.8284271247461903,
//    4.242640687119285,
//    5.656854249492381,
//    7.0710678118654755,
//    8.48528137423857,
//    9.899494936611665,
//    11.313708498984761,
//    12.727922061357856,
// ]
```

The long version is equivalent to the chained version, but it is more verbose.

Chaining Different Methods

Methods can be chained together to perform multiple operations on an array.

Example:

```javascript
// Filter out even numbers and double them
const evenDouble = numbers.filter((number) => {
  return number % 2 === 0;
}).map((number) => {
  return number * 2;
});

console.log(evenDouble); // [4, 8, 12, 16, 20]
```

In this example, we chain the filter() method to filter out the even numbers and the map() method to double each even number.

Reduce Method

The reduce() method reduces an array to a single value.

Example:

```javascript
// Calculate the total price of products in a shopping cart
const products = [
  { name: 'Product 1', price: 10 },
  { name: 'Product 2', price: 15 },
  { name: 'Product 3', price: 20 },
];

const totalPrice = products.reduce((total, product) => {
  return total + product.price;
}, 0);

console.log(totalPrice); // 45
```

In this example, we use the reduce() method to calculate the total price of the products in the shopping cart. The reduce() method takes two arguments: a callback function and an initial value. The callback function takes two arguments: the accumulator (total) and the current element (product). The accumulator is the value that is returned from the previous iteration of the callback function. The initial value is the starting value of the accumulator.

High-Order Array Methods : 145

The callback function adds the price of each product to the accumulator. The initial value is 0, so the accumulator starts at 0. After iterating through all the products, the accumulator will contain the total price of the products.

Example:

```javascript
// Calculate the sum of an array of numbers using a long
version of the callback function
const numbers = [1, 2, 3, 4, 5, 6, 7, 8, 9, 10];

const sum = numbers.reduce((accumulator, currentValue) => {
  return accumulator + currentValue;
}, 0);

console.log(sum); // 55
```

In this example, the accumulator starts at 0 (the initial value) and is updated with the sum of the accumulator and the current value on each iteration of the callback function.

Shorthand Version:

```javascript
// Calculate the sum of an array of numbers using a shorthand
version of the callback function
const sum2 = numbers.reduce((acc, cur) => acc + cur, 0);

console.log(sum2); // 55
```

Setting the Initial Value

The initial value can be set to any value. For example, if we want to start the accumulator at 10, we can do the following:

```javascript
const sum3 = numbers.reduce((acc, cur) => acc + cur, 10);

console.log(sum3); // 65
```

For Loop Equivalent

The following for loop is equivalent to the reduce() method example above:

```
let sum = 0;

for (let i = 0; i < numbers.length; i++) {
   sum += numbers[i];
}

console.log(sum); // 55
```

Reduce Method vs. For Loop

The reduce() method can be used to perform the same operations as a for loop. However, the reduce() method is often more concise and easier to read.

For Loop Example:

```
// Calculate the sum of an array of numbers using a for loop
const numbers = [1, 2, 3, 4, 5, 6, 7, 8, 9, 10];

let sum3 = 0;

for (const number of numbers) {
   sum3 += number;
}

console.log(sum3); // 55
```

Reduce Method Example:

```
// Calculate the sum of an array of numbers using the reduce() method
const sum4 = numbers.reduce((acc, cur) => acc + cur, 0);

console.log(sum4); // 55
```

As you can see, the reduce() method is more concise and easier to read than the for loop.

Shopping Cart :

Let's use the reduce() method to calculate the total price of a shopping cart:

```javascript
// Shopping cart array
const cart = [
  { id: 1, name: 'Product 1', price: 130 },
  { id: 2, name: 'Product 2', price: 150 },
  { id: 3, name: 'Product 3', price: 175 },
];

// Calculate the total price using the reduce() method
const total = cart.reduce((acc, product) => acc + product.price, 0);

console.log(total); // 455
```

In this example, the reduce() method is used to iterate over the cart array and add the price of each product to the accumulator. The initial value of the accumulator is set to 0. The result is the total price of the shopping cart.

Challenge

Create an Array of Young People

Instructions:

Given an array of people objects, create an array called `youngPeople` that stores objects with only the `name` and `email` properties of all the people that are under 25 years old. The `name` property should have their first and last name concatenated.

Example:

```
const people = [
  { firstName: 'Bob', lastName: 'Smith', email: 'bob@example.com', age: 45 },
  { firstName: 'Jane', lastName: 'Doe', email: 'jane@example.com', age: 25 },
  { firstName: 'John', lastName: 'Smith', email: 'john@example.com', age: 30 },
  { firstName: 'Jose', lastName: 'Garcia', email: 'jose@example.com', age: 22 },
];

const youngPeople = people
  .filter(person => person.age <= 25)
  .map(person => ({
    name: `${person.firstName} ${person.lastName}`,
    email: person.email,
  }));

console.log(youngPeople);
```

Output:

```
[
  { name: 'Jane Doe', email: 'jane@example.com' },
```

```
  { name: 'Jose Garcia', email: 'jose@example.com' },
]
```

1. We use the `filter()` method to create a new array that contains only the people who are under 25 years old.
2. We then use the `map()` method to create a new array that contains objects with only the `name` and `email` properties.
3. The `name` property is created by concatenating the first and last names of each person.
4. The `email` property is simply copied from the original object.

The result is an array of objects that contains only the `name` and `email` properties of the people who are under 25 years old.

Add All Positive Numbers

Instructions:

Given an array of numbers, add all the positive numbers in the array.

Example:

```
const numbers = [50, -20, 2, -7, 10];

const positiveSum = numbers
  .filter(number => number > 0)
  .reduce((accumulator, currentValue) => accumulator + currentValue, 0);

console.log(positiveSum); // 79
```

1. We use the `filter()` method to create a new array that contains only the positive numbers.
2. We then use the `reduce()` method to add all the numbers in the array.

3. The `reduce()` method takes two arguments: a callback function and an initial value.
4. The callback function takes two arguments: the accumulator and the current value.
5. The accumulator is the value that is returned from the previous iteration of the callback function.
6. The current value is the current element in the array.
7. In our example, the callback function simply adds the accumulator and the current value.
8. The initial value is the value that is used to start the reduction.
9. In our example, the initial value is 0.

The result is the sum of all the positive numbers in the array.

Capitalize First Letter of Words

Instructions:

Given an array of words, create a new array with the words from the original array but with the first letter of each word capitalized.

Example:

```
const words = ['coder', 'programmer', 'developer'];

const capitalizedWords = words.map(word => {
  return word[0].toUpperCase() + word.slice(1);
});

console.log(capitalizedWords); // ['Coder', 'Programmer', 'Developer']
```

1. We use the `map()` method to create a new array that contains the capitalized words.
2. The `map()` method takes a callback function as an argument.

3. The callback function takes a single argument: the current element in the array.
4. In our example, the callback function capitalizes the first letter of the word and then concatenates it with the rest of the word.
5. The result is an array of capitalized words.

Introduction to the Document Object Model (DOM)

What is the DOM?

The Document Object Model (DOM) is an interface that allows us to interact with page elements dynamically from a language like JavaScript.

Importance of Understanding the DOM

Before you jump into the DOM, you should have a good understanding of the fundamentals, including data types, functions, flow control, loops, and array methods.

What We Will Learn in This Section

In this section, we will look at:

- Properties and methods available on the document object
- Methods to select elements
- How to traverse the DOM
- How to change, add, and remove elements from the page dynamically
- How to change styles and attributes

Let's jump into the DOM and spend some time visualizing it. Then, we will look at the window object and its child object, the document object.

The DOM Tree Structure

The DOM is generally represented as a tree structure. Each HTML tag is represented as a node in the tree. Text between HTML tags is represented as text nodes.

Example:

The following HTML code:

Introduction to the Document Object Model (DOM)

```html
<html>
  <head>
    <title>My Page</title>
  </head>
  <body>
    <h1>Hello World</h1>
    <p>This is a paragraph.</p>
  </body>
</html>
```

Would be represented as the following DOM tree:

```
HTML
  HEAD
    TITLE
  BODY
    H1
    P
```

Accessing the DOM

We can access the DOM through the `window` object, which has a `document` property. The `document` object represents the entire HTML document.

Example:

```js
console.log(window.document);
```

Output:

```html
<html>
  <head>
    <title>My Page</title>
  </head>
  <body>
    <h1>Hello World</h1>
    <p>This is a paragraph.</p>
  </body>
</html>
```

Properties and Methods of the Document Object

The `document` object has a number of properties and methods that we can use to access and manipulate the DOM.

Accessing the Body and Its Contents

The `document.body` property represents the body element of the HTML document. We can use this property to access and manipulate the contents of the body.

Example:

```javascript
console.log(document.body); // Accesses the body element
console.log(document.body.innerHTML); // Accesses the HTML content of the body
console.log(document.body.innerText); // Accesses the text content of the body
```

Output:

```
<body>
 <h1>Hello World</h1>
 <p>This is a paragraph.</p>
</body>

<h1>Hello World</h1>
<p>This is a paragraph.</p>

Hello World
This is a paragraph.
```

Modifying the Body

We can modify the contents of the body using the `innerHTML` and `innerText` properties.

Example:

```javascript
document.body.innerHTML = "<h1>Hello World</h1>"; // Replaces the contents of the body with an H1 element
```

```js
document.body.innerText = "Hello World"; // Replaces the
contents of the body with the text "Hello World"
```

Output:

```
<h1>Hello World</h1>
Hello World
```

Accessing Links

The document.links property returns an HTML collection of all the links on the page. We can access each link by index.

Example:

```js
console.log(document.links); // Accesses all the links on the
page
console.log(document.links[0]); // Accesses the first link on
the page
```

Output:

```
HTMLCollection [a]
<a href="https://traversymedia.com" target="_blank">Traverse
Media</a>
```

Writing to the Document

The document.write() method writes the specified content to the document.

Example:

```js
document.write("Hello from JS"); // Writes "Hello from JS" to
the document
```

Output:

```
Hello from JS
```

Note:

The `document.write()` method is not commonly used because it overwrites the entire document. It is better to use methods like `createElement()` and `appendChild()` to insert content into the document.

Selecting Elements by ID

The `document.getElementById()` method returns the first element with the specified ID.

Example:

```javascript
const main = document.getElementById("main"); // Selects the element with the ID "main"
console.log(main); // Logs the selected element to the console
```

Output:

```html
<div id="main">
  <h1>Hello World</h1>
  <a href="https://traversymedia.com" target="_blank">Traverse Media</a>
</div>
```

We can modify the contents of an element by accessing its `innerHTML` property.

Example:

```javascript
main.innerHTML = "<h1>Hello from Main</h1>"; // Replaces the contents of the element with the ID "main" with an H1 element
console.log(main); // Logs the modified element to the console
```

Output:

```html
<div id="main">
  <h1>Hello from Main</h1>
</div>
```

Selecting Elements by Query Selector

The `document.querySelector()` method returns the first element that matches the specified selector.

Example:

```
const h1 = document.querySelector("#main h1"); // Selects the first H1 element within the element with the ID "main"
console.log(h1); // Logs the selected element to the console
```

Output:

```
<h1>Hello from Main</h1>
```

We can modify the contents of an element selected by query selector in the same way as we would modify an element selected by ID.

Example:

```
h1.innerText = "Hello from Query Selector"; // Replaces the text content of the H1 element selected by query selector
console.log(h1); // Logs the modified element to the console
```

Output:

```
<h1>Hello from Query Selector</h1>
```

The document object provides access to various properties that represent different parts of the HTML document.

Deprecated Properties:

- **`document.all`:** An HTMLAllCollection containing all elements in the document. This property is deprecated and should not be used.

Element Properties:

- **`document.documentElement`:** The root element of the document, typically the `<html>` element.

Introduction to the Document Object Model (DOM)

- **document.head:** The <head> element of the document.
- **document.body:** The <body> element of the document.

Child Collections:

- **.children:** A collection of the child elements of an element.

Example:

```javascript
// Get the HTMLAllCollection of all elements in the document
const allElements = document.all;

// Get the root element of the document
const htmlElement = document.documentElement;

// Get the head element of the document
const headElement = document.head;

// Get the body element of the document
const bodyElement = document.body;

// Get the child elements of the body element
const bodyChildren = bodyElement.children;
```

Output:

```
// allElements
[
  <html>,
  <head>,
  <body>,
  <script>,
  <meta>,
  <link>,
  <div>,
  ...
]

// htmlElement
<html>
```

```
<head>
   <meta>
   <link>
</head>
<body>
   <div>
      ...
   </div>
</body>
</html>

// headElement
<head>
   <meta>
   <link>
</head>

// bod yElement
<body>
   <div>
      ...
   </div>
</body>

// bodyChildren
[
   <div>
      ...
   </div>
]
```

Accessing Element Attributes

Elements in the DOM have various attributes that can be accessed and modified using JavaScript.

Getting Attributes:

- To get the value of an attribute, use the `dot` notation followed by the attribute name.
- For example, to get the `id` attribute of an element, use `element.id`.

Setting Attributes:

- To set the value of an attribute, use the `dot` notation followed by the attribute name and the assignment operator (=).
- For example, to set the `id` attribute of an element to "new-id", use `element.id = "new-id"`.

Example:

```javascript
// Get the ID of the form
const formId = document.forms[0].id;

// Set the ID of the form to "new-id"
document.forms[0].id = "new-id";

// Get the href attribute of the link
const linkHref = document.links[0].href;

// Set the ID of the link to "google-link"
document.links[0].id = "google-link";
```

Output:

```
// formId
"item-form"

// linkHref
"https://google.com"
```

Accessing and modifying element attributes is a common task in JavaScript, as it allows you to dynamically change the appearance and behavior of elements on the page.

Accessing Element Classes

Elements in the DOM can have multiple CSS classes assigned to them. JavaScript provides ways to access and modify these classes.

Getting Classes:

- To get a collection of all classes on an element, use the `classList` property.
- For example, to get the classes on an element, use `element.classList`.

Adding Classes:

- To add a class to an element, use the `classList.add()` method.
- For example, to add the class "google-class" to an element, use `element.classList.add("google-class")`.

Removing Classes:

- To remove a class from an element, use the `classList.remove()` method.
- For example, to remove the class "google-class" from an element, use `element.classList.remove("google-class")`.

Example:

```
// Get the classes on the link
const linkClasses = document.links[0].classList;

// Add the class "google-class" to the link
linkClasses.add("google-class");

// Remove the class "google-class" from the link
linkClasses.remove("google-class");
```

Output:

```
// linkClasses
DOMTokenList ["google-link"]
```

Accessing and modifying element classes is useful for dynamically changing the appearance and behavior of elements on the page based on user interactions or other conditions.

Accessing HTML Collections

HTML collections are array-like objects that represent a collection of elements in the DOM. They are returned by certain methods, such as `document.forms`, `document.links`, and `document.images`.

Properties:

- **length:** The number of elements in the collection.
- **item(index):** Returns the element at the specified index.

Example:

```
// Get the HTML collection of images
const images = document.images;

// Get the first image
const firstImage = images[0];

// Get the source of the first image
const firstImageSource = firstImage.src;
```

Output:

```
// firstImageSource
"note.png"
```

HTML collections are not true arrays, so they do not support all array methods. However, you can convert them to arrays using the `Array.from()` method.

Selecting Elements by ID

The `document.getElementById()` method allows you to select an element by its unique ID attribute.

Syntax:

```
document.getElementById(id);
```

Parameters:

- **id:** The ID of the element to select.

Example:

```
// Get the element with the ID "app-title"
const titleElement = document.getElementById("app-title");
```

Output:

```
// titleElement
<h1>Shopping List</h1>
```

Getting and Setting Attributes

Attributes are additional pieces of information that can be attached to elements. You can use JavaScript to get and set attributes.

Getting Attributes:

- To get an attribute, use the `getAttribute()` method.
- For example, to get the ID attribute of an element, use `element.getAttribute("id")`.

Setting Attributes:

- To set an attribute, use the `setAttribute()` method.
- For example, to set the title attribute of an element, use `element.setAttribute("title", "New Title")`.

Example:

```
// Get the title attribute of the title element
const title = titleElement.getAttribute("title");
```

```javascript
// Set the title attribute of the title element
titleElement.setAttribute("title", "Updated Title");
```

Output:

```
// title
"Shopping List"
```

Note:

Getting and setting attributes is useful for dynamically changing the appearance and behavior of elements on the page based on user interactions or other conditions.

Manipulating Element Content and Styles

Once you have selected an element, you can manipulate its content and styles using JavaScript.

Getting and Setting Content:

- To get the text content of an element, use the `textContent` property.
- To set the text content, use the `textContent` property with an assignment operator.

Example:

```javascript
// Get the text content of the title element
const titleText = titleElement.textContent;

// Set the text content of the title element
titleElement.textContent = "Hello World";
```

Output:

```
// titleText
"Shopping List"
```

Getting and Setting HTML:

- To get the HTML content of an element, use the `innerHTML` property.
- To set the HTML content, use the `innerHTML` property with an assignment operator.

Example:

```javascript
// Get the HTML content of the title element
const titleHTML = titleElement.innerHTML;

// Set the HTML content of the title element
titleElement.innerHTML = "<strong>Shopping List</strong>";
```

Output:

```
// titleHTML
"Shopping List"
```

Modifying Styles:

- To modify the styles of an element, use the `style` property.
- The `style` property is an object that allows you to set CSS properties.

Example:

```javascript
// Set the color of the title element to red
titleElement.style.color = "red";

// Set the background color of the title element to black
titleElement.style.backgroundColor = "black";
```

Output:

The title element will have its text color changed to red and its background color changed to black.

Manipulating element content and styles is essential for creating dynamic and interactive web pages. You can use these techniques to change the appearance and behavior of elements based on user interactions or other conditions.

Query Selector

document.querySelector() is a powerful selector that allows you to select a single element from the DOM based on a specified selector. It is similar to document.getElementById() and document.getElementsByClassName(), but it is more versatile and can select elements based on a wider range of criteria.

Syntax:

document.querySelector(selector);

Parameters:

- selector: A CSS selector that specifies the element to be selected.

Return Value:

- The first element that matches the specified selector, or null if no element is found.

Example:

```
// Select the first H1 element
const h1Element = document.querySelector("h1");

// Select the element with the ID "app-title"
const titleElement = document.querySelector("#app-title");

// Select the first input element with a type of "text"
const textInputElement = document.querySelector("input[type=text]");

// Select the second list item
const secondListItem = document.querySelector("li:nth-child(2)");
```

Output:

```
// h1Element
<h1>Shopping List</h1>

// titleElement
<h1>Shopping List</h1>

// textInputElement
<input type="text" placeholder="Enter a task">

// secondListItem
<li>Orange Juice</li>
```

Advantages:

- **Versatility:** Can select elements based on a wide range of criteria, including ID, class, attribute, and pseudo-selectors.
- **Simplicity:** Easy to use and understand.
- **Performance:** Faster than document.getElementById() and document.getElementsByClassName() in most cases.

document.querySelector() is a powerful tool for selecting elements from the DOM. It is essential for manipulating the content and styles of web pages dynamically.

Query Selector All

document.querySelectorAll() is a method that allows you to select all elements that match a specified selector. It is similar to document.querySelector(), but it returns an array of all matching elements instead of just the first one.

Syntax:

```
document.querySelectorAll(selector);
```

Parameters:

- **selector**: A CSS selector that specifies the elements to be selected.

Return Value:

- An array of all elements that match the specified selector.

Example:

```
// Select all list items
const listItems = document.querySelectorAll("li");

// Select all elements with a class of "item"
const itemElements = document.querySelectorAll(".item");
```

Output:

```
// listItems
[<li>Apples</li>, <li>Orange Juice</li>, <li>Oreos</li>, <li>Milk</li>]

// itemElements
[<li class="item">Apples</li>, <li class="item">Orange Juice</li>, <li class="item">Oreos</li>, <li class="item">Milk</li>]
```

Advantages:

- **Selects multiple elements:** Can select all elements that match a specified selector, regardless of their position in the DOM.
- **Returns an array:** Provides an array of matching elements, which can be easily iterated over.
- **Versatile:** Can select elements based on a wide range of criteria, including ID, class, attribute, and pseudo-selectors.

`document.querySelectorAll()` is a powerful tool for selecting multiple elements from the DOM. It is essential for manipulating the content and styles of web pages dynamically.

Node Lists vs HTML Collections

`document.querySelectorAll()` returns a node list, which is an array-like structure that contains the matching elements. Node lists are similar to HTML collections, which are returned by older methods like `document.getElementsByTagName()` and `document.getElementsByClassName()`.

Key Differences:

- **Array-like vs. Array:** Node lists are array-like, meaning they have a length property and can be iterated over using a for loop. However, they are not true arrays and do not have all the methods of arrays.
- **High-Order Array Methods:** You can use high-order array methods (e.g., `map()`, `filter()`, `reduce()`) on node lists. This is not possible with HTML collections.
- **Accessing Individual Elements:** You can access individual elements in a node list using the bracket syntax (e.g., `listItems[1]`).

Example:

```
// Select all list items
const listItems = document.querySelectorAll("li");

// Iterate over the node list using a for loop
for (let i = 0; i < listItems.length; i++) {
  console.log(listItems[i]);
}
```

Output:

```
<li>Apples</li>
<li>Orange Juice</li>
<li>Oreos</li>
<li>Milk</li>
```

Introduction to the Document Object Model (DOM)

You can manipulate node lists using the same methods as arrays. For example, you can use `forEach()` to iterate over the elements and perform actions on each one.

```javascript
// Change the color of all list items to red
listItems.forEach((item) => {
  item.style.color = "red";
});
```

It is important to understand the differences between node lists and HTML collections when working with JavaScript. Node lists are more versatile and allow for more advanced manipulation.

Additional Notes:

- You can convert an HTML collection to an array using the `Array.from()` method.
- You can use `document.querySelectorAll()` to select elements that are nested within other elements.
- You can use `document.querySelectorAll()` to select elements that are not visible on the page.

Converting HTML Collections to Arrays

To use high-order array methods or other array-specific functionality, you can convert an HTML collection to an array using the `Array.from()` method.

```javascript
// Convert the HTML collection to an array
const listItemsArray = Array.from(listItems);

// Use high-order array methods on the array
listItemsArray.forEach((item) => {
  console.log(item);
});
```

It is important to understand the differences between HTML collections and node lists when working with JavaScript. Node lists are more versatile and allow for more advanced manipulation.

Traversing the DOM: Parent, Child, and Sibling Relationships

Once you have selected an element from the DOM, you can use its properties to navigate and traverse the DOM tree. These properties allow you to access the parent element, child elements, and sibling elements of the selected element.

Key Properties:

- **parentElement:** Returns the parent element of the selected element.
- **firstElementChild:** Returns the first child element of the selected element.
- **lastElementChild:** Returns the last child element of the selected element.
- **nextElementSibling:** Returns the next sibling element of the selected element.
- **previousElementSibling:** Returns the previous sibling element of the selected element.
- **children:** Returns a node list of all the child elements of the selected element.

Example:

```
// Select the parent element
const parent = document.querySelector(".parent");

// Get the first child element
const firstChild = parent.firstElementChild;

// Get the last child element
const lastChild = parent.lastElementChild;
```

```javascript
// Get the next sibling element
const nextSibling = firstChild.nextElementSibling;

// Get the previous sibling element
const previousSibling = lastChild.previousElementSibling;

// Get all child elements
const children = parent.children;
```

Output:

```
firstChild: <div class="child">Child 1</div>
lastChild: <div class="child">Child 3</div>
nextSibling: <div class="child">Child 2</div>
previousSibling: <div class="child">Child 2</div>
children: [
  <div class="child">Child 1</div>,
  <div class="child">Child 2</div>,
  <div class="child">Child 3</div>
]
```

These properties are useful for traversing the DOM tree and manipulating elements based on their relationships.

Modifying Elements and Traversing the DOM

Once you have selected an element from the DOM, you can use its properties to modify its content and style. You can also use these properties to traverse the DOM tree and access parent and sibling elements.

Modifying Elements:

- You can use the `textContent` or `innerText` property to change the text content of an element.
- You can use the `style` property to modify the style of an element.

Example:

```javascript
// Select the first child element
const firstChild = document.querySelector(".child");

// Change the text content
firstChild.textContent = "Child One";

// Add a border to the parent element
firstChild.parentElement.style.border = "1px solid #ccc";
```

Traversing the DOM:

- You can use the `parentElement` property to access the parent element of an element.
- You can use the `firstElementChild` and `lastElementChild` properties to access the first and last child elements of an element.
- You can use the `nextElementSibling` and `previousElementSibling` properties to access the next and previous sibling elements of an element.

Example:

```javascript
// Select the second child element
const secondChild = document.querySelector(".child:nth-child(2)");

// Access the parent element
const parent = secondChild.parentElement;

// Access the next sibling element
const nextSibling = secondChild.nextElementSibling;
```

These properties are useful for manipulating elements and navigating the DOM tree.

Traversing the DOM: Sibling Elements

You can use the `nextElementSibling` and `previousElementSibling` properties to access the next and previous sibling elements of an element.

Example:

```javascript
// Select the second child element
const secondChild = document.querySelector(".child:nth-child(2)");

// Access the next sibling element
const nextSibling = secondChild.nextElementSibling;

// Access the previous sibling element
const previousSibling = secondChild.previousElementSibling;
```

Traversing the DOM: Other Node Types

In addition to element nodes, there are other types of nodes in the DOM, such as text nodes, attribute nodes, and comment nodes. You can use the following properties to traverse these different types of nodes:

- `parentNode`: Returns the parent node of the current node.
- `childNodes`: Returns a list of all child nodes of the current node.
- `firstChild`: Returns the first child node of the current node.
- `lastChild`: Returns the last child node of the current node.
- `nextSibling`: Returns the next sibling node of the current node.
- `previousSibling`: Returns the previous sibling node of the current node.

Example:

```javascript
// Select the first child element
const firstChild = document.querySelector(".child");

// Access the parent node
const parentNode = firstChild.parentNode;
```

```javascript
// Access the first child node
const firstChildNode = parentNode.firstChild;
```

Note:

These properties work with all types of nodes, not just element nodes.

Traversing the DOM: Child Nodes

The `childNodes` property returns a list of all child nodes of a given node. This includes all types of nodes, not just element nodes.

Example:

```javascript
// Select the parent element
const parentElement = document.querySelector(".parent");

// Access the child nodes
const childNodes = parentElement.childNodes;

// Log the child nodes to the console
console.log(childNodes);
```

Output:

```
[
  #text,
  <!-- Children -->,
  <div class="child">...</div>,
  #text,
  <div class="child">...</div>,
  #text,
  <div class="child">...</div>,
  #text
]
```

Comments as Nodes

Comments are considered to be a specific type of node in the DOM. They can be accessed using the `childNodes` property.

Example:

```javascript
// Select the parent element
const parentElement = document.querySelector(".parent");

// Access the child nodes
const childNodes = parentElement.childNodes;

// Find the comment node
const commentNode = childNodes[1];

// Log the comment node to the console
console.log(commentNode);
```

Output:

```
<!-- Children -->
```

Accessing Node Properties

Each node in the DOM has a number of properties that provide information about the node. These properties include:

- `nodeType`: The type of node (e.g., element, text, comment).
- `nodeName`: The name of the node (e.g., "DIV", "P", "#text").
- `textContent`: The text content of the node.
- `innerHTML`: The HTML content of the node.
- `outerHTML`: The HTML content of the node and its children.

Example:

```javascript
// Select the first child node
const childNode = parentElement.childNodes[0];

// Access the node properties
console.log(childNode.nodeType); // 1 (element node)
console.log(childNode.nodeName); // "DIV"
console.log(childNode.textContent); // "Child One"
```

```
console.log(childNode.innerHTML); // "Child One"
console.log(childNode.outerHTML); // "<div>Child One</div>"
```

Output:

```
1
DIV
Child One
Child One
<div>Child One</div>
```

Accessing Parent Nodes

The parentNode property returns the parent node of a given node.

Example:

```
// Select the child node
const childNode = parentElement.childNodes[0];

// Access the parent node
const parentNode = childNode.parentNode;

// Log the parent node to the console
console.log(parentNode);
```

Output:

```
<div class="parent">...</div>
```

Note:

- The parentNode property can be used to navigate up the DOM tree.
- You can use the parentNode property to access the parent element of a node.

Accessing Siblings

The `nextSibling` and `previousSibling` properties return the next and previous sibling nodes of a given node, respectively.

Example:

```javascript
// Select the second child node
const secondChildNode = parentElement.childNodes[1];

// Access the next sibling node
const nextSiblingNode = secondChildNode.nextSibling;

// Access the previous sibling node
const previousSiblingNode = secondChildNode.previousSibling;

// Log the sibling nodes to the console
console.log(nextSiblingNode); // Text node
console.log(previousSiblingNode); // Text node
```

Output:

#text
#text

Note:

- The `nextSibling` and `previousSibling` properties can be used to navigate across the DOM tree.
- You can use the `nextSibling` and `previousSibling` properties to access the next and previous element nodes of a node.

Creating Elements

The `createElement()` method creates a new element node of the specified type.

Example:

```javascript
// Create a new div element
const newDiv = document.createElement("div");

// Log the new div element to the console
console.log(newDiv);
```

Output:

`<div></div>`

Note:

- The `createElement()` method can be used to create any type of element node.
- The new element node is not added to the DOM until it is appended to a parent node.

Adding Content to Elements

There are two main ways to add content to an element:

- **Using `innerText`:** This property sets the text content of an element. However, it is not recommended to use `innerText` when creating new elements, as it can overwrite existing content.
- **Using `appendChild()`:** This method appends a child node to an element. You can use this method to append text nodes, element nodes, or other types of nodes.

Example:

```javascript
// Create a new div element
const newDiv = document.createElement("div");

// Create a new text node
const newTextNode = document.createTextNode("Hello world");

// Append the text node to the div element
newDiv.appendChild(newTextNode);
```

```
// Append the div element to the body
document.body.appendChild(newDiv);
```

Output:

The "Hello world" text will be displayed at the bottom of the page.

Note:

- The `appendChild()` method can be used to insert nodes at any position within an element.
- You can also use the `insertBefore()` method to insert nodes before a specific child node.

Creating a Function to Add List Items

In this example, we will create a function called `createListItem()` that takes an item as an argument and adds a new list item to the shopping list. We will demonstrate two ways to do this:

- **Using `innerHTML`:** This method sets the HTML content of an element. It is a quick and easy way to add content, but it is not recommended for creating new elements.
- **Using `createElement()` and `appendChild()`:** This method is more performant and allows you to create and append new elements to the DOM.

Example:

Using `innerHTML`:

```
function createListItem(item) {
  const li = document.createElement("li");
  li.innerHTML = `<span>${item}</span><button><i class="fas fa-trash"></i></button>`;
  document.querySelector("ul.items").appendChild(li);
}
```

In the previous example, we used the `innerHTML` method to add a new list item to the shopping list. While this method is quick and easy, it is not recommended for creating new elements because it can overwrite existing content and make it difficult to maintain your code.

A better approach is to create each element individually using the `createElement()` method and then append them to the DOM using the `appendChild()` method. This method is more performant and allows you to have more control over the structure of your elements.

Example:

```javascript
function createListItem(item) {
  // Create the list item element
  const li = document.createElement("li");

  // Create the text node for the list item
  const textNode = document.createTextNode(item);

  // Append the text node to the list item
  li.appendChild(textNode);

  // Create the button element
  const button = document.createElement("button");

  // Add classes to the button
  button.classList.add("btn", "btn-danger");

  // Create the icon element
  const i = document.createElement("i");

  // Add classes to the icon
  i.classList.add("fas", "fa-trash");

  // Append the icon to the button
  button.appendChild(i);

  // Append the button to the list item
  li.appendChild(button);

  // Append the list item to the DOM
```

```javascript
    document.querySelector("ul.items").appendChild(li);
}
```

Output:

This code will create a new list item with the specified item name and a button with a trash icon. The list item will be appended to the shopping list.

Advantages of Using `createElement()` and `appendChild()`:

- **Performance:** Creating elements individually and appending them to the DOM is more performant than using `innerHTML`.
- **Control:** You have more control over the structure of your elements when you create them individually.
- **Event handlers:** Event handlers will be automatically reattached to new elements when you create them individually.

Note:

- The `createTextNode()` method creates a text node that contains the specified text.
- The `classList` property allows you to add or remove classes from an element.
- The `appendChild()` method appends a node to the end of the specified parent node.

Creating Reusable Functions for Elements

In the previous example, we created a single function called `createListItem()` that handled the creation of the list item, button, and icon. While this approach is functional, it can become difficult to maintain as your codebase grows.

A better approach is to create separate functions for each element. This makes your code more modular and reusable.

Example:

```javascript
// Create a function to create a button
function createButton(classes) {
  // Create the button element
  const button = document.createElement("button");

  // Add classes to the button
  button.classList.add(...classes);

  // Return the button
  return button;
}

// Create a function to create an icon
function createIcon(classes) {
  // Create the icon element
  const i = document.createElement("i");

  // Add classes to the icon
  i.classList.add(...classes);

  // Return the icon
  return i;
}

// Create a function to create a list item
function createListItem(item) {
  // Create the list item element
  const li = document.createElement("li");

  // Create the text node for the list item
  const textNode = document.createTextNode(item);

  // Append the text node to the list item
  li.appendChild(textNode);

  // Create the button
  const button = createButton(["btn", "btn-danger"]);
```

```javascript
// Create the icon
const icon = createIcon(["fas", "fa-trash"]);

// Append the icon to the button
button.appendChild(icon);

// Append the button to the list item
li.appendChild(button);

// Append the list item to the DOM
document.querySelector("ul.items").appendChild(li);
}
```

This code will create a new list item with the specified item name, a button with a trash icon, and a separate function for creating the button and icon.

Advantages of Using Separate Functions:

- **Modularity:** Separate functions make your code easier to maintain and understand.
- **Reusability:** You can reuse the `createButton()` and `createIcon()` functions in other parts of your code.
- **Flexibility:** You can easily customize the button and icon by passing different classes to the functions.

Note:

- The `classList` property allows you to add or remove classes from an element.
- The `...` spread operator allows you to pass an array of classes to the `classList.add()` method.
- The `appendChild()` method appends a node to the end of the specified parent node.

Inserting Elements into the DOM

In addition to `appendChild()`, there are several other methods you can use to insert elements into the DOM. These methods allow you to insert elements before, after, or within a specified reference element.

Insert Adjacent Element

The `insertAdjacentElement()` method takes two arguments:

- **position:** A string specifying where to insert the new element. Possible values are:
    - beforebegin: Before the reference element
    - afterbegin: Inside the reference element, at the beginning
    - beforeend: Inside the reference element, at the end
    - afterend: After the reference element
- **element:** The new element to insert

Example:

```javascript
// Insert an H1 element before the filter form
const filterForm = document.querySelector(".filter");
const h1 = document.createElement("h1");
h1.textContent = "Insert Adjacent Element";
filterForm.insertAdjacentElement("beforebegin", h1);
```

Insert Adjacent Text

The `insertAdjacentText()` method is similar to `insertAdjacentElement()`, but it inserts text instead of an element.

Example:

```javascript
// Insert the text "Hello World" before the filter form
const filterForm = document.querySelector(".filter");
filterForm.insertAdjacentText("beforebegin", "Hello World");
```

Advantages of Using Insert Adjacent Methods:

- **Flexibility:** You can insert elements or text before, after, or within a specified reference element.
- **Control:** You have precise control over the position of the inserted content.
- **Efficiency:** These methods are generally more efficient than using `appendChild()` or `insertBefore()`.

Note:

- The `insertAdjacentElement()` and `insertAdjacentText()` methods are supported by all major browsers.
- The `position` argument must be one of the four specified values.
- The `element` argument must be a valid DOM element.

In addition to the `insertAdjacentElement()` and `insertAdjacentText()` methods, you can also use the `insertAdjacentHTML()` method to insert HTML content.

Example:

```javascript
// Insert an H2 element before the clear button
const clearBtn = document.querySelector("#clear");
clearBtn.insertAdjacentHTML("beforebegin", "<h2>Insert Adjacent HTML</h2>");
```

insertBefore() Method

The `insertBefore()` method is similar to `appendChild()`, but it allows you to insert an element before a specified reference element.

Example:

```javascript
// Insert a new list item before the third list item
const ul = document.querySelector("ul");
const thirdItem = ul.querySelector("li:nth-child(3)");
const newItem = document.createElement("li");
newItem.textContent = "New Item";
ul.insertBefore(newItem, thirdItem);
```

Advantages of Using `insertBefore()`:

- **Control:** You have precise control over the position of the inserted element.
- **Efficiency:** `insertBefore()` is generally more efficient than using `appendChild()` or `insertAdjacentElement()`.

Note:

- The `insertAdjacentHTML()` method is supported by all major browsers.
- The `insertBefore()` method is supported by all major browsers except for Internet Explorer 9 and below.
- The `referenceNode` argument must be a valid DOM element.

Comparison of `insertAdjacent` and `insertBefore`

Method	Inserts	Position
`insertAdjacentElement()`	Element	Before, after, or within a reference element
`insertAdjacentText()`	Text	Before, after, or within a reference element
`insertAdjacentHTML()`	HTML	Before, after, or within a reference element
`insertBefore()`	Element	Before a reference element

Which Method to Use?

- Use `insertAdjacentElement()`, `insertAdjacentText()`, or `insertAdjacentHTML()` when you need to insert content before, after, or within a specified reference element.
- Use `insertBefore()` when you need to insert an element before a specified reference element.

Since JavaScript does not provide an `insertAfter()` method, you can create your own custom function to achieve this functionality.

Example:

```
// Custom insertAfter function
function insertAfter(newElement, existingElement) {
  // Get the parent element of the existing element
  const parentElement = existingElement.parentElement;

  // Insert the new element after the existing element
  parentElement.insertBefore(newElement, existingElement.nextSibling);
}
```

How it Works:

- The `insertAfter()` function takes two parameters: `newElement` (the element to be inserted) and `existingElement` (the element after which the new element should be inserted).
- It retrieves the parent element of the `existingElement` using the `parentElement` property.
- It then uses the `insertBefore()` method to insert the `newElement` after the `existingElement`. The `nextSibling` property is used to get the element after the `existingElement`.

Usage:

```
// Create a new list item
const newItem = document.createElement("li");
newItem.textContent = "New Item";

// Insert the new item after the first list item
insertAfter(newItem, document.querySelector("li:first-child"));
```

Advantages of Using a Custom `insertAfter()` Function:

- **Flexibility:** You can customize the function to meet your specific needs.
- **Control:** You have precise control over the position of the inserted element.
- **Efficiency:** The custom function can be more efficient than using multiple DOM methods.

Note:

- The `insertAfter()` function is not supported by any major browsers.
- It is recommended to use the `insertBefore()` method with a reference element to achieve the same result.

Replacing Elements in the DOM

Once you have mastered inserting elements into the DOM, you can move on to replacing existing elements. There are several methods available for this purpose.

Example 1: Using `replaceWith()`

```
// Function to replace the first list item
function replaceFirstItem() {
  // Get the first list item
  const firstItem = document.querySelector("li:first-child");

  // Create a new list item to replace it
  const newItem = document.createElement("li");
  newItem.textContent = "Replaced First";

  // Replace the first item with the new item
  firstItem.replaceWith(newItem);
}
```

How it Works:

- The `replaceFirstItem()` function selects the first list item using `querySelector()`.

- It creates a new list item with the text content "Replaced First".
- It then calls the `replaceWith()` method on the first item, passing in the new item. This replaces the first item with the new item.

Example 2: Using outerHTML

```
// Function to replace the second list item
function replaceSecondItem() {
  // Get the second list item
  const secondItem = document.querySelector("li:nth-child(2)");

  // Create a new list item to replace it
  const newItem = document.createElement("li");
  newItem.textContent = "Replaced Second";

  // Replace the second item with the new item using outerHTML
  secondItem.outerHTML = newItem.outerHTML;
}
```

How it Works:

- The `replaceSecondItem()` function selects the second list item using `querySelector()`.
- It creates a new list item with the text content "Replaced Second".
- It then sets the `outerHTML` property of the second item to the `outerHTML` of the new item. This replaces the second item with the new item.

Advantages of Using `replaceWith()` and `outerHTML`:

- **Simplicity:** Both methods provide a straightforward way to replace elements.
- **Efficiency:** They are relatively efficient compared to other methods.

- **Flexibility:** outerHTML allows you to replace an element with any valid HTML, including elements with event listeners and other attributes.

To replace all items in a list, you can use a loop to iterate through each item and set its outerHTML property.

Example:

```javascript
// Function to replace all list items
function replaceAllItems() {
  // Get all list items
  const lis = document.querySelectorAll("li");

  // Loop through the list items
  lis.forEach((item, index) => {
    // Set the outerHTML of each item to "Replace All"
    item.outerHTML = `<li>Replace All</li>`;
  });
}
```

How it Works:

- The replaceAllItems() function selects all list items using querySelectorAll().
- It then uses forEach() to iterate through the list items.
- For each item, it sets the outerHTML property to a new list item with the text content "Replace All".

Replacing a Specific Item

You can also use the forEach() loop to replace a specific item in the list.

Example:

```javascript
// Function to replace the second list item
function replaceSecondItem() {
  // Get all list items
  const lis = document.querySelectorAll("li");
```

```
// Loop through the list items
lis.forEach((item, index) => {
    // If the index is equal to 1 (the second item), set the outerHTML to "Replace Second"
    if (index === 1) {
        item.outerHTML = `<li>Replace Second</li>`;
    }
});
}
```

How it Works:

- The replaceSecondItem() function selects all list items using querySelectorAll().
- It then uses forEach() to iterate through the list items.
- For each item, it checks if the index is equal to 1 (the second item).
- If the index is equal to 1, it sets the outerHTML property to a new list item with the text content "Replace Second".

Advantages of Using forEach():

- **Flexibility:** You can use forEach() to perform any operation on each item in the list.
- **Efficiency:** forEach() is a relatively efficient way to iterate through a list.
- **Simplicity:** The syntax for forEach() is straightforward and easy to understand.

Replacing an Element with a New Element

To replace an element with a new element, you can select the parent element, select the element you want to replace, and then replace it with the new element.

Example:

```javascript
// Function to replace the H1 with an H2
function replaceChildHeading() {
  // Select the header element
  const header = document.querySelector("header");

  // Select the H1 element
  const h1 = header.querySelector("h1");

  // Create a new H2 element
  const h2 = document.createElement("h2");

  // Set the ID of the H2 element
  h2.id = "app-title";

  // Set the text content of the H2 element
  h2.textContent = "Shopping List";

  // Replace the H1 element with the H2 element
  header.replaceChild(h2, h1);
}
```

How it Works:

- The `replaceChildHeading()` function selects the header element using `querySelector()`.
- It then selects the H1 element within the header using `querySelector()`.
- It creates a new H2 element using `createElement()`.
- It sets the ID and text content of the H2 element.
- Finally, it replaces the H1 element with the H2 element using `replaceChild()`.

Advantages of Using `replaceChild()`:

- **Simplicity:** The syntax for `replaceChild()` is straightforward and easy to understand.
- **Efficiency:** `replaceChild()` is a relatively efficient way to replace an element.

- **Flexibility:** You can use `replaceChild()` to replace any element with any other element.

Removing Elements

To remove an element, you can use the `remove()` method on the element you want to remove. To remove a child element, you can use the `removeChild()` method on the parent element.

Example:

```
// Function to remove the clear button
function removeClearButton() {
  // Select the clear button
  const clearButton = document.querySelector("#clear");

  // Remove the clear button
  clearButton.remove();
}

// Function to remove the first list item
function removeFirstItem() {
  // Select the UL element
  const ul = document.querySelector("ul");

  // Select the first list item
  const li = ul.querySelector("li");

  // Remove the first list item
  ul.removeChild(li);
}
```

How it Works:

- The `removeClearButton()` function selects the clear button using `querySelector()`.

- It then calls the `remove()` method on the clear button to remove it from the DOM.
- The `removeFirstItem()` function selects the UL element and the first list item within the UL element using `querySelector()`.
- It then calls the `removeChild()` method on the UL element to remove the first list item.

Advantages of Using `remove()` and `removeChild()`:

- **Simplicity:** The syntax for `remove()` and `removeChild()` is straightforward and easy to understand.
- **Efficiency:** `remove()` and `removeChild()` are relatively efficient ways to remove elements.
- **Flexibility:** You can use `remove()` and `removeChild()` to remove any element from the DOM.

Removing a Specific Item from a List

To remove a specific item from a list, you can use the `removeChild()` method on the parent element. However, if you know the index of the item you want to remove, you can use the `nth-child` pseudo-selector to select the item and then use the `remove()` method to remove it.

Example 1: Using `removeChild()`

```
// Function to remove the item at a specific index
function removeItem(itemNumber) {
  // Select the UL element
  const ul = document.querySelector("ul");

  // Select the LI element at the specified index
  const li = ul.querySelector(`li:nth-child(${itemNumber})`);

  // Remove the LI element
  ul.removeChild(li);
}
```

How it Works:

- The `removeItem()` function selects the UL element using `querySelector()`.
- It then selects the LI element at the specified index using the `nth-child` pseudo-selector.
- Finally, it removes the LI element using `removeChild()`.

Example 2: Using `remove()`

```javascript
// Function to remove the item at a specific index
function removeItem2(itemNumber) {
  // Select all LI elements
  const lis = document.querySelectorAll("li");

  // Remove the LI element at the specified index
  lis[itemNumber - 1].remove();
}
```

How it Works:

- The `removeItem2()` function selects all LI elements using `querySelectorAll()`.
- It then removes the LI element at the specified index using the `remove()` method.
- Note that the index is zero-based, so you need to subtract 1 from the item number to get the correct index.

Advantages of Using `removeChild()` and `remove()`:

- **Simplicity:** The syntax for `removeChild()` and `remove()` is straightforward and easy to understand.
- **Efficiency:** `removeChild()` and `remove()` are relatively efficient ways to remove elements.
- **Flexibility:** You can use `removeChild()` and `remove()` to remove any element from the DOM.

Manipulating CSS Classes and Styles

JavaScript provides several properties and methods that allow you to manipulate CSS classes and styles dynamically. These properties and methods can be used to add, remove, or modify CSS classes and styles, giving you greater control over the appearance and behavior of your web pages.

Example: Using `className`

```
// Select the item list
const itemList = document.querySelector(".item-list");

// Log the class name of the item list
console.log(itemList.className); // Output: "item-list"
```

How it Works:

- The `className` property returns the class name of the specified element.
- In this example, we select the item list using `querySelector()` and then log its class name to the console.

Other Properties and Methods:

- **classList:** A property that provides a list of the element's CSS classes.
- **classList.add():** Adds one or more CSS classes to the element.
- **classList.remove():** Removes one or more CSS classes from the element.
- **classList.toggle():** Adds a CSS class if it doesn't exist, or removes it if it does.
- **style:** A property that allows you to access and modify the inline styles of the element.

Advantages of Using JavaScript to Manipulate CSS:

- **Dynamic Control:** JavaScript allows you to change CSS classes and styles dynamically, based on user interactions or other events.
- **Flexibility:** You can use JavaScript to apply complex styling rules that would be difficult or impossible to achieve with CSS alone.
- **Improved Performance:** By using JavaScript to manipulate CSS, you can avoid unnecessary page reloads and improve the performance of your web pages.

Manipulating CSS Classes with `classList`

The `classList` property provides a more advanced way to manipulate CSS classes. It allows you to add, remove, or toggle classes without overwriting existing classes.

Example: Using `classList.add()`

```javascript
// Select the paragraph
const paragraph = document.querySelector("p");

// Add the "dark" class to the paragraph
paragraph.classList.add("dark");
```

How it Works:

- The `classList.add()` method adds one or more CSS classes to the element.
- In this example, we select the paragraph and add the "dark" class to it.

Other `classList` Methods:

- **classList.remove():** Removes one or more CSS classes from the element.
- **classList.toggle():** Adds a CSS class if it doesn't exist, or removes it if it does.

- **classList.replace()**: Replaces one CSS class with another.

Advantages of Using `classList`:

- **Precise Control:** `classList` allows you to add, remove, or toggle specific CSS classes without affecting other classes.
- **Improved Performance:** By using `classList`, you can avoid unnecessary class name overwriting, which can improve the performance of your web pages.
- **Flexibility:** `classList` provides a range of methods that make it easy to manipulate CSS classes dynamically.

Example: Using `classList.toggle()`

```javascript
// Select the paragraph
const paragraph = document.querySelector("p");

// Toggle the "hidden" class on the paragraph
paragraph.classList.toggle("hidden");
```

How it Works:

- The `classList.toggle()` method adds a CSS class if it doesn't exist, or removes it if it does.
- In this example, we toggle the "hidden" class on the paragraph, which will hide or show it depending on its current state.

Styling Elements with `style` Property

The `style` property allows you to directly manipulate the CSS styles of an element. You can use it to set or change any CSS property.

Example: Setting Line Height

```javascript
// Select the item list
const itemList = document.querySelector("ul");
```

```javascript
// Set the line height to 3
itemList.style.lineHeight = "3";
```

How it Works:

- The `style` property is an object that contains all the CSS properties of the element.
- In this example, we select the item list and set the `lineHeight` property to "3".

Looping Through Elements and Styling

```javascript
// Select all list items
const items = document.querySelectorAll("li");

// Loop through the list items
items.forEach((item, index) => {
  // Set the color to red
  item.style.color = "red";

  // If the index is 2, set the color to blue
  if (index === 2) {
    item.style.color = "blue";
  }
});
```

How it Works:

- The `querySelectorAll()` method returns a list of all elements matching the selector.
- We loop through the list items using `forEach()`, and for each item, we set the color to red.
- If the index of the item is 2, we set the color to blue.

Event Listeners

Event listeners are used to listen for specific actions or events that occur on an element. When an event occurs, the event listener triggers a callback function that executes the desired action.

Recommended Method: addEventListener()

The recommended method for adding event listeners is to use the addEventListener() method. This method takes two arguments:

- **Event Type:** The type of event to listen for, such as "click" or "keydown".
- **Callback Function:** The function to execute when the event occurs.

Example: Adding a Click Event Listener

```javascript
// Select the clear button
const clearBtn = document.querySelector("#clear");

// Add a click event listener
clearBtn.addEventListener("click", () => {
  alert("Clear items");
});
```

How it Works:

- We select the clear button using querySelector().
- We call the addEventListener() method on the clear button, specifying the "click" event type and an anonymous arrow function as the callback.
- When the clear button is clicked, the callback function is executed, displaying an alert box with the message "Clear items".

Multiple Event Listeners

You can add multiple event listeners to the same element for different events. For example, we can add another event listener to the clear button to log a message to the console:

```
clearBtn.addEventListener("click", () => {
  alert("Clear items");
});

clearBtn.addEventListener("click", () => {
  console.log("Clear items");
});
```

Advantages of `addEventListener()`

- **Flexibility:** Allows you to add multiple event listeners to the same element.
- **Separation of Concerns:** Keeps HTML and JavaScript code separate, making it easier to maintain.
- **Cross-Browser Compatibility:** Supported by all major browsers.

Multiple Event Listeners with Different Actions

Using `addEventListener()`, you can add multiple event listeners to the same element that perform different actions. For example, we can add a click event listener that displays an alert and another that logs a message to the console:

```
clearBtn.addEventListener("click", () => {
  alert("Clear items");
});

clearBtn.addEventListener("click", () => {
  console.log("Clear items");
});
```

Synchronous vs. Asynchronous Execution

When an event listener is triggered, the callback function is executed. If the callback function is a blocking operation, such as an alert, it will prevent other code from executing until it is complete. In the example above, the alert box will block the execution of the console log until it is closed.

Named Callback Functions

Instead of using anonymous arrow functions as callbacks, you can use named functions. When using named functions, do not include parentheses when passing them as arguments to `addEventListener()`.

```
function onClear() {
  alert("Clear items");
}

clearBtn.addEventListener("click", onClear);
```

Removing Event Listeners

To remove an event listener, use the `removeEventListener()` method. This is useful when removing elements from the DOM.

```
setTimeout(() => {
  clearBtn.removeEventListener("click", onClear);
}, 5000);
```

Triggering Events Programmatically

You can trigger an event programmatically using the `dispatchEvent()` method. This can be useful for testing or simulating user interactions.

```
setTimeout(() => {
  clearBtn.dispatchEvent(new Event("click"));
}, 5000);
```

Clearing Items from a List

Now that we have a clear button, let's make it actually clear the items from the list. There are several ways to do this:

1. Setting Inner HTML to Empty

```
const itemList = document.querySelector("ul");
clearBtn.addEventListener("click", () => {
  itemList.innerHTML = "";
});
```

2. Looping Through and Removing List Items

```
const itemList = document.querySelector("ul");
const items = itemList.querySelectorAll("li");
clearBtn.addEventListener("click", () => {
  items.forEach((item) => {
    item.remove();
  });
});
```

3. Using a While Loop

```
const itemList = document.querySelector("ul");
clearBtn.addEventListener("click", () => {
  while (itemList.firstChild) {
    itemList.removeChild(itemList.firstChild);
  }
});
```

The while loop is generally considered the most performant method for removing multiple items from a list.

Other Mouse Events

In addition to the `click` event, there are several other mouse events that we can listen for:

Double Click
```
logo.addEventListener("dblclick", () => {
  console.log("Double click event");
  if (body.style.backgroundColor !== "purple") {
    body.style.backgroundColor = "purple";
    body.style.color = "white";
  } else {
    body.style.backgroundColor = "white";
    body.style.color = "black";
  }
});
```

Context Menu
```
logo.addEventListener("contextmenu", (e) => {
  e.preventDefault(); // Prevent the default context menu from opening
  console.log("Context menu event");
});
```

The `contextmenu` event is triggered when the user right-clicks on an element. By calling `e.preventDefault()`, we can prevent the default context menu from opening.

Mouse Over and Mouse Out
```
logo.addEventListener("mouseover", () => {
  console.log("Mouse over event");
});

logo.addEventListener("mouseout", () => {
  console.log("Mouse out event");
});
```

The `mouseover` event is triggered when the mouse cursor enters an element, while the `mouseout` event is triggered when the mouse cursor leaves an element.

Mouse Move
```
logo.addEventListener("mousemove", (e) => {
  console.log(`Mouse move event: ${e.clientX}, $
```

```
{e.clientY}`);
});
```

The `mousemove` event is triggered when the mouse cursor moves within an element. The `e.clientX` and `e.clientY` properties provide the X and Y coordinates of the mouse cursor relative to the document.

Right Click
```
logo.addEventListener("contextmenu", (e) => {
  e.preventDefault(); // Prevent the default context menu from opening
  console.log("Right click event");
});
```

The `contextmenu` event is triggered when the user right-clicks on an element. By calling `e.preventDefault()`, we can prevent the default context menu from opening.

Mouse Down and Mouse Up
```
logo.addEventListener("mousedown", () => {
  console.log("Mouse down event");
});

logo.addEventListener("mouseup", () => {
  console.log("Mouse up event");
});
```

The `mousedown` event is triggered when the user presses down on the mouse button, while the `mouseup` event is triggered when the user releases the mouse button.

Mouse Wheel
```
logo.addEventListener("wheel", (e) => {
  console.log("Mouse wheel event");
});
```

The `wheel` event is triggered when the user scrolls the mouse wheel.

Mouse Over and Mouse Out

```
logo.addEventListener("mouseover", () => {
  console.log("Mouse over event");
});

logo.addEventListener("mouseout", () => {
  console.log("Mouse out event");
});
```

The `mouseover` event is triggered when the mouse cursor enters an element, while the `mouseout` event is triggered when the mouse cursor leaves an element.

Drag Start

```
logo.addEventListener("dragstart", () => {
  console.log("Drag start event");
});
```

The `dragstart` event is triggered when the user starts dragging an element.

Drag and Drag End

```
logo.addEventListener("drag", () => {
  console.log("Drag event");
});

logo.addEventListener("dragend", () => {
  console.log("Drag end event");
});
```

The `drag` event is triggered continuously while the user is dragging an element. The `dragend` event is triggered when the user stops dragging an element.

Event Object

When an event is triggered, an event object is created and passed to the event handler function. This object contains information about the event, such as the target element, the type of event, and the coordinates of the mouse cursor.

To access the event object, we can use the e parameter in the event handler function. For example:

```
logo.addEventListener("click", (e) => {
  console.log(e.target); // The element that triggered the event
  console.log(e.type); // The type of event
  console.log(e.clientX); // The X coordinate of the mouse cursor
  console.log(e.clientY); // The Y coordinate of the mouse cursor
});
```

Target vs. Current Target

The `target` property of the event object refers to the element that triggered the event, while the `currentTarget` property refers to the element that the event listener is attached to.

In most cases, the `target` and `currentTarget` properties will be the same. However, there are some exceptions. For example, if an event bubbles up through the DOM tree, the `target` property will refer to the element that triggered the event, while the `currentTarget` property will refer to the element that the event listener is attached to.

To illustrate this difference, let's add an event listener to the body element:

```
document.body.addEventListener("click", (e) => {
  console.log("Target:", e.target);
  console.log("Current Target:", e.currentTarget);
});
```

Now, if we click on a list item within the body, we will see that the `target` property refers to the list item, while the `currentTarget` property refers to the body element. This is because the click event bubbles up from the list item to the body element.

Other Event Object Properties

In addition to `target` and `currentTarget`, the event object also contains a number of other properties, including:

- `type`: The type of event that was triggered.
- `timestamp`: The time at which the event was triggered.
- `clientX` and `clientY`: The X and Y coordinates of the mouse cursor relative to the window.

These properties can be useful for getting information about the event and the element that triggered it. For example, we could use the `clientX` and `clientY` properties to determine where the user clicked on an element.

Mouse Coordinates

The event object also contains a number of properties that provide information about the position of the mouse cursor. These properties include:

- `clientX` and `clientY`: The X and Y coordinates of the mouse cursor relative to the window.
- `offsetX` and `offsetY`: The X and Y coordinates of the mouse cursor relative to the element that triggered the event.
- `pageX` and `pageY`: The X and Y coordinates of the mouse cursor relative to the page.
- `screenX` and `screenY`: The X and Y coordinates of the mouse cursor relative to the entire screen.

These properties can be useful for getting information about where the user clicked on an element or for tracking the movement of the mouse cursor.

Preventing Default Behavior

The `preventDefault()` method can be used to prevent the default behavior of an event. For example, if an event is triggered on a form element, the default behavior is for the form to be submitted. However, we can use `preventDefault()` to stop the form from being submitted.

This can be useful for validating form data before submitting it or for handling form submissions with JavaScript.

To illustrate how to use `preventDefault()`, let's add an event listener to the link in our HTML document:

```javascript
document.querySelector("a").addEventListener("click", (e) =>
{
  e.preventDefault();
  console.log("Link was clicked");
});
```

Now, when we click on the link, the default behavior of navigating to the linked page will be prevented. Instead, the "Link was clicked" message will be logged to the console.

Dynamic Event Values

Some event properties, such as `clientX` and `clientY`, can change dynamically. For example, if we have a drag event, the `clientX` and `clientY` properties will constantly change as the mouse cursor moves.

To illustrate this, let's add an event listener to the logo element that listens for the `drag` event:

```javascript
logo.addEventListener("drag", (e) => {
  const h1 = document.querySelector("h1");
  h1.textContent = `X: ${e.clientX}, Y: ${e.clientY}`;
});
```

Now, when we drag the logo element, the `textContent` of the h1 element will change to display the current X and Y coordinates of the mouse cursor.

This demonstrates how we can use event properties to create dynamic and interactive web applications, especially games.

Keyboard Events

Keyboard events allow us to detect when a key is pressed, released, or held down. There are three main keyboard events:

- **keypress:** Fired when a key is pressed.
- **keyup:** Fired when a key is released.
- **keydown:** Fired when a key is pressed and held down.

To listen for keyboard events, we can use the `addEventListener()` method on an element. For example, to listen for the `keypress` event on the `itemInput` element, we can use the following code:

```
itemInput.addEventListener("keypress", (e) => {
  console.log("Key press");
});
```

Key Properties

The `event` object for keyboard events contains several properties that provide information about the key that was pressed. These properties include:

- **key:** The name of the key that was pressed (e.g., "Enter", "A", "ArrowUp").
- **keyCode:** The numeric code for the key that was pressed (e.g., 13 for Enter, 65 for A, 38 for ArrowUp).
- **code:** A newer property that provides a more standardized representation of the key that was pressed (e.g., "Enter", "KeyA", "ArrowUp").
- **repeat:** A boolean value that indicates whether the key is being held down.

We can use these properties to determine which key was pressed and take appropriate action. For example, we could use the following code to display an alert when the Enter key is pressed:

```javascript
itemInput.addEventListener("keypress", (e) => {
  if (e.key === "Enter") {
    alert("Enter key pressed");
  }
});
```

Using Key Codes

We can use the `keyCode` property to check for specific keys. For example, to check if the Enter key was pressed, we can use the following code:

```javascript
itemInput.addEventListener("keypress", (e) => {
  if (e.keyCode === 13) {
    alert("Enter key pressed");
  }
});
```

Using the Repeat Property

The `repeat` property can be used to determine if a key is being held down. This can be useful for creating games or other applications where we need to know how long a key has been pressed. For example, we could use the following code to display a message when a key is held down for more than 1 second:

```javascript
itemInput.addEventListener("keydown", (e) => {
  if (e.repeat) {
    console.log("Key is being held down");
  }
});
```

Modifier Keys

The `event` object for keyboard events also contains properties that indicate whether the Shift, Control, or Alt keys are being pressed. These properties are:

- **shiftKey:** A boolean value that indicates whether the Shift key is being pressed.

- **ctrlKey:** A boolean value that indicates whether the Control key is being pressed.
- **altKey:** A boolean value that indicates whether the Alt key is being pressed.

We can use these properties to check for modifier key combinations. For example, to check if the Control key and the letter "A" are being pressed, we can use the following code:

```
itemInput.addEventListener("keypress", (e) => {
  if (e.ctrlKey && e.key === "a") {
    alert("Control + A pressed");
  }
});
```

Using Modifier Keys with Key Codes

We can combine the `keyCode` property with the modifier key properties to check for specific key combinations. For example, to check if the Shift key is being pressed and the letter "K" is being pressed, we can use the following code:

```
itemInput.addEventListener("keypress", (e) => {
  if (e.shiftKey && e.keyCode === 75) {
    console.log("Shift + K pressed");
  }
});
```

Building a Key Code Info Application

Now that we have a good understanding of keyboard events and key codes, let's build a simple application that displays the key code, key, and code properties for any key that is pressed.

Method 1: Using Hard-Coded HTML

The simplest way to create this application is to use hard-coded HTML to create the three display elements:

```html
<div id="key-code">Key Code:</div>
<div id="key">Key:</div>
<div id="code">Code:</div>
```

Then, we can add an event listener to the window object to listen for keypress events:

```javascript
window.addEventListener("keypress", (e) => {
  document.getElementById("key-code").innerHTML = e.keyCode;
  document.getElementById("key").innerHTML = e.key;
  document.getElementById("code").innerHTML = e.code;
});
```

Method 2: Using Dynamically Created Elements

A more performant and flexible approach is to create the display elements dynamically using JavaScript. This allows us to easily add or remove elements as needed.

```javascript
// Create the display elements
const keyCodeElement = document.createElement("div");
const keyElement = document.createElement("div");
const codeElement = document.createElement("div");

// Set the element IDs
keyCodeElement.id = "key-code";
keyElement.id = "key";
codeElement.id = "code";

// Add the elements to the DOM
document.body.appendChild(keyCodeElement);
document.body.appendChild(keyElement);
document.body.appendChild(codeElement);

// Add the event listener to the window object
window.addEventListener("keypress", (e) => {
  keyCodeElement.innerHTML = e.keyCode;
  keyElement.innerHTML = e.key;
  codeElement.innerHTML = e.code;
});
```

Event Listeners

Both of these methods will create a simple application that displays the key code, key, and code properties for any key that is pressed.

Dynamically Creating Display Elements

In the previous method, we used hard-coded HTML to create the display elements. However, a more flexible and performant approach is to create the elements dynamically using JavaScript. This allows us to easily add or remove elements as needed.

To do this, we can use the following steps:

Create the display elements using the `createElement()` method:
```
const keyCodeElement = document.createElement("div");
const keyElement = document.createElement("div");
const codeElement = document.createElement("div");
```

Set the element IDs:
```
keyCodeElement.id = "key-code";
keyElement.id = "key";
codeElement.id = "code";
```

Add the elements to the DOM using the `appendChild()` method:
```
document.body.appendChild(keyCodeElement);
document.body.appendChild(keyElement);
document.body.appendChild(codeElement);
```

Update the inner HTML of the elements to display the key code, key, and code properties:
```
keyCodeElement.innerHTML = e.keyCode;
keyElement.innerHTML = e.key;
codeElement.innerHTML = e.code;
```

This method gives us more control over the display elements and allows us to easily update them as needed.

Handling the Space Key

One thing to note is that the space key has a key property of an empty string. To handle this, we can use a conditional statement to check if the key property is empty and, if so, display the word "space" instead:

```
if (e.key === "") {
  keyElement.innerHTML = "space";
} else {
  keyElement.innerHTML = e.key;
}
```

This ensures that the space key is displayed correctly in the application.

Creating Display Elements Dynamically Using an Object Map

Instead of using hard-coded HTML, we can create the display elements dynamically using an object map. This allows us to easily add or remove elements as needed and provides more control over the display.

To do this, we can use the following steps:

Create an object map to store the key-value pairs for the display elements:
```
const keyCodes = {
  "key": e.key,
  "key code": e.keyCode,
  "code": e.code
};
```

Loop through the object map using a `for...in` loop:
```
for (let key in keyCodes) {
  // Create a div element for each key-value pair
  const div = document.createElement("div");
  div.classList.add("key");

  // Create a small element for the key-value pair
  const small = document.createElement("small");

  // Set the text content of the small element to the key-
```

value pair
```
  small.textContent = keyCodes[key];

  // Append the small element to the div
  div.appendChild(small);

  // Append the div to the insert element
  insert.appendChild(div);
}
```

This method gives us more flexibility and control over the display elements, allowing us to easily add or remove elements as needed.

Creating Display Elements Dynamically Using Text Nodes

To create the display elements dynamically, we can use text nodes to set the content of the elements. This allows us to easily update the display without having to recreate the elements themselves.

To do this, we can use the following steps:

Create a text node for the key:
```
const keyText = document.createTextNode(key);
```

Create a text node for the value:
```
const valueText = document.createTextNode(keyCodes[key]);
```

Append the text nodes to the elements:
```
small.appendChild(keyText);
div.appendChild(valueText);
```

This method gives us more control over the display elements and allows us to easily update the content as needed.

To prevent the display from becoming cluttered, we can clear the inner HTML of the insert element before adding new elements:

```
insert.innerHTML = "";
```

This ensures that only the most recent key press is displayed.

Handling Input Events

In addition to key events, we can also handle input events to get the values for form inputs. This allows us to interact with form elements and retrieve the user's input.

To handle input events, we can use the following steps:

1. Get the input element:

```
const input = document.getElementById("priority-input");
```

2. Add an event listener for the input event:

```
input.addEventListener("input", (e) => {
  // Get the value of the input
  const value = e.target.value;

  // Do something with the value
});
```

This allows us to get the value of the input element whenever it changes and perform any necessary actions.

Retrieving Input Values Using Event Listeners

To retrieve the values of form inputs, we can use event listeners to handle input events. This allows us to get the value of the input whenever it changes.

To do this, we can use the following steps:

1. Get the input element:

```
const itemInput = document.getElementById("item-input");
```

2. Add an event listener for the input event:

```
itemInput.addEventListener("input", (e) => {
  // Get the value of the input
  const value = e.target.value;

  // Do something with the value
});
```

Event Listeners

The `input` event is fired whenever the value of the input changes. This allows us to get the value of the input in real time.

To get the value of an input element, we can use the `value` property of the `target` element:

```
const value = e.target.value;
```

This gives us the current value of the input element.

Updating the Display Dynamically

We can use the value of the input element to update the display dynamically. For example, we can update the text content of a heading to show the current value of the input:

```
heading.textContent = value;
```

This allows us to create dynamic displays that update in real time as the user types.

Retrieving Values from Select Lists and Checkboxes

Select lists and checkboxes have slightly different ways of retrieving their values.

Select Lists

For select lists, we can still use the `input` event to get the value. The `e.target.value` property will give us the value of the selected option.

```
priorityInput.addEventListener("input", (e) => {
  const value = e.target.value;

  // Do something with the value
});
```

Checkboxes

For checkboxes, we can use the `change` event instead of the `input` event. The `e.target.checked` property will give us a boolean value indicating whether the checkbox is checked or not.

```javascript
checkBox.addEventListener("change", (e) => {
  const isChecked = e.target.checked;

  // Do something with the value
});
```

Focus and Blur Events

The `focus` and `blur` events are used to detect when an input element is focused or blurred (unfocused). These events can be useful for adding visual effects or changing the behavior of the input.

```javascript
itemInput.addEventListener("focus", (e) => {
  // Input is focused
});

itemInput.addEventListener("blur", (e) => {
  // Input is blurred
});
```

Example: Dynamically Updating the Display

We can use the values of the input elements to dynamically update the display. For example, we can update the text content of a heading to show the current value of the checkbox:

```javascript
heading.textContent = isChecked ? "Checked" : "Not checked";
```

This allows us to create dynamic displays that update in real time as the user interacts with the input elements.

Styling Input Elements with Focus and Blur

The `focus` and `blur` events can also be used to dynamically change the styling of input elements. For example, we can add an outline to an input when it is focused and remove it when it is blurred.

```
itemInput.addEventListener("focus", (e) => {
  itemInput.style.outlineStyle = "solid";
  itemInput.style.outlineWidth = "1px";
  itemInput.style.outlineColor = "green";
});

itemInput.addEventListener("blur", (e) => {
  itemInput.style.outlineStyle = "none";
});
```

This allows us to create visual effects that enhance the user experience and make the input elements more interactive.

Preventing Form Submission

When a form is submitted, it typically sends the data to a server-side script for processing. However, in JavaScript, we can prevent the form from submitting and handle the data ourselves.

To prevent form submission, we can use the `preventDefault()` method on the `submit` event.

```
itemForm.addEventListener("submit", (e) => {
  e.preventDefault();

  // Do something with the form data
});
```

This allows us to keep the form data on the client-side and process it using JavaScript, without sending it to a server.

Form Validation and Data Retrieval

Once we have prevented the form from submitting, we can retrieve the data from the form fields and validate it.

There are two ways to retrieve form data:

Using the `value` property: We can access the value of an input field using the `value` property. For example:

```js
const item = document.getElementById("item-input").value;
const priority = document.getElementById("priority-input").value;
```

Using the `FormData` object: The `FormData` object provides a more convenient way to retrieve form data. We can create a `FormData` object by passing the form element to its constructor. For example:

```js
const formData = new FormData(itemForm);
```

The `FormData` object has a `get()` method that we can use to retrieve the value of a form field using the input name. For example:

```js
const item = formData.get("item");
const priority = formData.get("priority");
```

Once we have retrieved the form data, we can validate it. For example, we can check if the `item` field is empty or if the `priority` field is set to its default value. If either of these conditions is true, we can display an error message and prevent the form from submitting.

```js
if (!item || priority === "0") {
  alert("Please fill in all fields");
  return;
}
```

If the form data is valid, we can proceed to process it using JavaScript.

We can also use the `entries()` method to retrieve all of the entries in the form data. The `entries()` method returns an iterator, which we can use to loop through the entries.

```js
for (const entry of formData.entries()) {
  console.log(entry);
}
```

Each entry is an array with two elements: the name of the form field and the value of the form field.

```
[
  ["item", "milk"],
```

```
["priority", "1"]
]
```

The `FormData` object is a powerful tool for retrieving form data. It is more convenient to use than the `value` property, and it provides a way to retrieve all of the form data in one go.

Event Bubbling

When an event occurs on an element, it bubbles up the DOM tree. This means that if an event listener is attached to a parent element, the event will be fired on that element as well.

For example, if we add an event listener to the `button` element, the event will also be fired on the `div` element and the `form` element.

```
<form>
  <div>
    <button>Click me</button>
  </div>
</form>
document.querySelector("button").addEventListener("click", () => {
  console.log("Button clicked");
});

document.querySelector("div").addEventListener("click", () => {
  console.log("Div clicked");
});

document.querySelector("form").addEventListener("click", () => {
  console.log("Form clicked");
});
```

If we click on the button, all three event listeners will be fired.

```
Button clicked
Div clicked
Form clicked
```

Event bubbling can be useful for handling events that can occur on multiple elements. For example, we could add an event listener to the document element to handle all clicks on the page.

```
document.addEventListener("click", (event) => {
  // Handle the click event
});
```

However, event bubbling can also be a problem. For example, if we have a nested list of elements, and we add an event listener to the parent element, the event will be fired on all of the child elements as well.

```
<ul>
  <li>Item 1</li>
  <li>Item 2</li>
  <li>Item 3</li>
</ul>
```

```
document.querySelector("ul").addEventListener("click", () => {
  console.log("List item clicked");
});
```

If we click on any of the list items, the event listener will be fired three times.

```
List item clicked
List item clicked
List item clicked
```

To prevent event bubbling, we can use the `stopPropagation()` method. The `stopPropagation()` method stops the event from bubbling up the DOM tree.

```
document.querySelector("ul").addEventListener("click", (event) => {
  event.stopPropagation();
```

```
    console.log("List item clicked");
});
```

Now, if we click on any of the list items, the event listener will only be fired once.

```
List item clicked
```

Event Delegation

Event delegation is a technique that can be used to improve the performance of event handling. Event delegation involves attaching an event listener to a parent element, and then using the `event.target` property to determine which child element triggered the event.

For example, instead of adding an event listener to each list item, we could add an event listener to the `ul` element.

```
document.querySelector("ul").addEventListener("click",
(event) => {
  const target = event.target;

  if (target.tagName === "LI") {
    console.log("List item clicked");
  }
});
```

This approach is more efficient because it only requires one event listener to be attached to the DOM.

Example

Let's say we have a list of items, and we want to add a delete button to each item. We could add an event listener to each delete button, but this would be inefficient. Instead, we can use event delegation to add a single event listener to the parent element (the `ul` element).

```
<ul>
  <li>Item 1 <button>Delete</button></li>
  <li>Item 2 <button>Delete</button></li>
```

```
  <li>Item 3 <button>Delete</button></li>
</ul>

document.querySelector("ul").addEventListener("click",
(event) => {
  const target = event.target;

  if (target.tagName === "BUTTON") {
    const li = target.parentNode;
    li.remove();
  }
});
```

When the user clicks on a delete button, the `event.target` property will be set to the delete button. We can then use the `parentNode` property to get the parent element (the `li` element), and then remove the `li` element from the DOM.

Event delegation is a powerful technique that can be used to improve the performance of event handling. It is especially useful when you have a large number of elements that you want to add event listeners to.

In the previous example, we used event delegation to add a click event listener to a parent element (`ul`), and then used the `event.target` property to determine which child element (the `li` element) was clicked.

We can use the same technique to add event listeners for other events, such as mouseover events.

```
document.querySelector("ul").addEventListener("mouseover",
(event) => {
  const target = event.target;

  if (target.tagName === "LI") {
    target.style.color = "red";
  }
});
```

When the user hovers over a list item, the `event.target` property will be set to the list item. We can then use the `style` property to change the color of the list item to red.

Window Events

The `window` object is a global object that represents the browser window. The `window` object has a number of properties and methods, including event listeners.

One common use of window events is to listen for page loading events. For example, we can use the `onload` event to run code after the page has finished loading.

```
window.onload = function() {
    // Code to be executed after the page has finished loading
};
```

Another common use of window events is to listen for browser events, such as resizing the window or scrolling the page. For example, we can use the `onresize` event to run code when the window is resized.

```
window.onresize = function() {
    // Code to be executed when the window is resized
};
```

Window events are a powerful way to interact with the browser and the page. They can be used to add functionality to your web pages, such as responding to user input or changing the appearance of the page.

In addition `onload` event, we can also use the `DOMContentLoaded` event to listen for page loading events. The `DOMContentLoaded` event fires when the HTML document has been parsed and the DOM has been built, but before any images or other resources have been loaded.

```
window.addEventListener("DOMContentLoaded", function() {
    // Code to be executed when the DOM has been loaded
});
```

The `DOMContentLoaded` event is often used to run code that manipulates the DOM, such as adding event listeners or changing the appearance of the page.

In addition to page loading events, we can also listen for other events on the `window` object, such as the `resize` event. The `resize` event fires when the browser window is resized.

```javascript
window.addEventListener("resize", function() {
  // Code to be executed when the window is resized
});
```

The `resize` event can be used to update the layout of the page or to perform other tasks that need to be done when the window is resized.

Window events are a powerful way to interact with the browser and the page. They can be used to add functionality to your web pages, such as responding to user input or changing the appearance of the page.

In addition to the `resize` event, we can also listen for other events on the `window` object, such as the `scroll` event. The `scroll` event fires when the browser window is scrolled.

```javascript
window.addEventListener("scroll", function() {
  // Code to be executed when the window is scrolled
});
```

The `scroll` event can be used to update the layout of the page or to perform other tasks that need to be done when the window is scrolled.

For example, we can use the `scroll` event to change the appearance of the page as the user scrolls down.

```javascript
window.addEventListener("scroll", function() {
  if (window.scrollY > 70) {
    document.body.style.backgroundColor = "black";
    document.body.style.color = "white";
  } else {
```

```
    document.body.style.backgroundColor = "white";
    document.body.style.color = "black";
  }
});
```

This code will change the background color of the page to black and the text color to white when the user scrolls down more than 70 pixels. When the user scrolls back up, the background color and text color will change back to white and black, respectively.

Focus and Blur Events

The `focus` and `blur` events are fired when an element gains or loses focus, respectively. These events can be used to add functionality to your web pages, such as validating input or changing the appearance of an element.

For example, we can use the `focus` and `blur` events to change the color of all paragraphs on the page when the user clicks in and out of them.

```
document.querySelectorAll("p").forEach(function(p) {
  p.addEventListener("focus", function() {
    p.style.color = "blue";
  });

  p.addEventListener("blur", function() {
    p.style.color = "black";
  });
});
```

This code will change the color of all paragraphs on the page to blue when the user clicks in them, and back to black when the user clicks out of them.

Window events and focus/blur events are powerful tools that can be used to add functionality and interactivity to your web pages.

Deferring Script Execution

As we mentioned earlier, it is generally considered best practice to place script tags at the bottom of the page, just before the closing `</body>` tag. This ensures that the DOM has been fully loaded before the JavaScript code is executed.

However, there are times when it may be necessary to place script tags in the `<head>` of the document. In these cases, we can use the `defer` attribute to defer the execution of the script until the DOM has been loaded.

```
<script defer src="my-script.js"></script>
```

The `defer` attribute tells the browser to download the script immediately, but to wait until the DOM has been loaded before executing it. This allows us to place scripts in the `<head>` of the document without blocking the rendering of the page.

www.ingramcontent.com/pod-product-compliance
Lightning Source LLC
Chambersburg PA
CBHW050052230526
45470CB00004B/1490